IMAGES OF

HUNGARIAN ARMOURED FIGHTING VEHICLES IN THE SECOND WORLD WAR

EDUARDO MANUEL GIL MARTÍNEZ

TRANSLATOR: RICARDO RAMALLO GIL

Pen & Sword

MILITARY

AN IMPRINT OF PEN & SWORD BOOKS LTD.
YORKSHIRE – PHILADELPHIA

First published in Great Britain in 2019 by
PEN & SWORD MILITARY
An imprint of
Pen & Sword Books Ltd
Yorkshire - Philadelphia

Copyright © Eduardo Manuel Gil Martínez, 2019

ISBN 978 1 52675 381 6

Typeset in Gill Sans 12/14 by
Aura Technology and Software Services, India

Printed and bound in India
By Replika Press Pvt. Ltd.

Pen & Sword Books Ltd incorporates the Imprints of Pen & Sword Books Archaeology, Atlas, Aviation, Battleground, Discovery, Family History, History, Maritime, Military, Naval, Politics, Railways, Select, Transport, True Crime, Fiction, Frontline Books, Leo Cooper, Praetorian Press, Seaforth Publishing, Wharncliffe and White Owl.

For a complete list of Pen & Sword titles please contact

PEN & SWORD BOOKS LIMITED
47 Church Street, Barnsley, South Yorkshire, S70 2AS, England
E-mail: enquiries@pen-and-sword.co.uk
Website: www.pen-and-sword.co.uk

or

PEN AND SWORD BOOKS
1950 Lawrence Rd, Havertown, PA 19083, USA
E-mail: uspen-and-sword@casematepublishers.com

Dedicated to:
Solete (my life)
My parents Salud y Eduardo.
Merce, Caco y Ricardo.
Ángel y sus nietos June, Iñigo e Ibón.

Acknowledgments for their invaluable help in bringing
this work to fruition: Péter Mujzer, B. Stenge Czaba, Károly "Karika"
Nemeth, Sean Lambert and Fortepan.

Contents

Introduction

Even many of those who are well-versed in the history of the period know only a little of the performance of the armoured forces of Germany's allies during the Second World War. Although the part they played was often quite tangential, it would be worth remembering the courageous behaviour of the Hungarian armoured forces. In recent times, authors such as Péter Mujzer, Czaba Becze, Clotier or Bernád and Climent have added a great deal to our knowledge of this topic. This book will hopefully bring the highlights of the intervention of the Hungarian armoured forces during the Second World War to a wider public.

Chapter One

The Birth of the Hungarian Armoured Forces

The history of Hungarian armour during the Second World War was marked by the secondary role to which Germany relegated its European allies. Advances in military technology during the years of the war were so fast that the industry of Hungary, Romania and Italy could not at any time be at the same level of development reached by the Soviet or American war machine, nor could they equal their output. This caused a great dependence on the German industry to support them, but the circumstances of the war prevented this support being sufficient for these satellite countries to keep up with their Soviet rival.

The obsolete Hungarian Fiat 3000B tanks did not participate in the armed conflict due to their obsolescence, although in this photo taken in 1942 they were still in service. The Renault FT-17 became the model for the Fiat 3000, the second Italian design model. Production had first begun in May 1919. FORTEPAN 39454 Tarbay Julia.

Despite its significant limitations, the Hungarian industry managed to put into action a Hungarian-made armoured force to which various types of vehicles of Czech or German origin would be added, eventually making Hungary the most reliable German ally because of their virtual self-sufficiency in this field.

At the end of the First World War, the Austro-Hungarian Empire was split among several countries, subject to the conditions of the Treaty of Versailles in 1919 and Austrian territory was reduced further by the Treaty of Trianon in 1920. The Hungarian armed forces were radically limited in quantity and in the quality of their materials; besides this, Hungary lost part of Transylvania (which passed to Romania), Rijeka, Slovakia, Croatia, Vojvodina or Bosnia-Herzegovina.

The situation worsened for Hungary when in the 1930s, all its neighbours (Czechoslovakia, Romania or Yugoslavia) developed more quickly than Hungary, leaving the country partly surrounded and vulnerable.

In 1934, Hungary improved its war potential with the acquisition of 150 tankettes, CV-33 Fiat-Ansaldos of Italian origin, and 12 armoured vehicles, Fiat L2s. Nicholas Strausser emerges as a major force in the design of armoured vehicles at this time. Strausser was a Hungarian who designed an armoured

Only one prototype of the Hungarian Straussler V4 vehicle was made and the line was not continued. In 1937, the Hungarian government carried out tests on three models of light tanks (Straussler V4, the German Pz I and the Swedish Landsverk L-60) to choose which one would be the standard tank of its armoured forces to be manufactured in Hungary, the winner being Landsverk L-60. Courtesy of Károly Németh.

vehicle, the Csaba, based on the Alvis C2 armed with a 20 mm cannon. The Honved (Royal Hungarian Army) placed an order of 100 units with the Hungarian company Manfred Weiss.

First blood

In 1938, as a result of Germany's territorial demands on Czechoslovakia, Hungary took the opportunity to claim part of its lost territories following the First World War. Before the opening of hostilities in November, northern Hungary was occupied peacefully by four infantry corps, with additional auxiliary units.

After that, Hungary's new objective was Ruthenia (part of the territory that also having been Hungarian, became part of Czechoslovakia in 1919) despite opposition from the Third Reich. The campaign began on 15 March 15 1939 with the attack by an advance guard of the VIII Army. The Hungarian onslaught was so fast, that on the 17th the companies equipped with Hungarian Ansaldo tankettes reached the Polish border. In ten days, the Hungarian objectives were achieved.

Inevitably during these actions, the Ansaldo tankettes clashed with a far more powerful enemy and the struggle continued for two weeks. Mechanical problems, breakdowns and lack of spare parts, undermined the success of these vehicles.

A Hungarian soldier poses proudly next to an Italian-painted Ansaldo tank. This Italian tank was developed in 1935 by Fiat and was popularly known as the Ansaldo. It had two 8mm machine guns. Approximately 120 units served under the Hungarian flag (152 according to Becze). Despite the high expectations when first put in the field, it was quickly clear that it was extremely vulnerable in combat. Courtesy of Károly Németh and Péter Mujzer.

After clashes over the annexation of part of Slovakia, the Hungarian army could see first-hand the importance of having adequate anti-aircraft protection. As well as this, taking into account the creation of a fast moving force, the anti-aircraft protection had to keep pace with it. The result was the Nimrod. It adequately provided anti-aircraft-anti-tank cover despite only having a 40-mm calibre gun, thanks to its high rate of fire. The Nimrod in the picture has the 'helmet' or driver hatch opened. Courtesy of Péter Mujzer.

A close-up of the narrow compartment for the crew of a Csaba tank. In 1939, 61 of these were ordered, followed by 20 more in the following year, although the latter were 40M Csaba, built in command version. This last model lacked a barrel, so its turret was smaller, but it had more powerful radio equipment. The final production run between 1939-44 totalled 145 vehicles, 105 39 M and 40 40 M. FORTEPAN LUDOVIKA.

Chapter Two

The Second World War Begins

At the beginning of the war, the Hungarian Army consisted of nine Corps, one Mobile Corps, twenty-five divisions and eighteen regiments, as well as other mixed frontier units. Among them the Mobile Corps deserves special mention, as the corps of the army which included two motorized brigades and two cavalry brigades apart from other minor units. The motorised troops had motorcycles and motorcycles with sidecars that increased the Hungarian off-road capability.

The start of the war allowed Hungary to throw off the shackles of the Treaty of Trianon. The army began to grow very fast because, since the end of the First World War no limitations had been imposed on army recruitment, so a mere restructuring was all that was necessary. It was, however, more necessary to acquire better and more up-to-date military equipment, both internally and from abroad. Germany and Italy were the main suppliers, using their own materials and that of the war booty of the conquered countries. In fact, after the German attack on Poland, nineteen Polish tanks fleeing from the enemy arrived in Hungary, so they were interned and then used by the army.

Hungary took advantage of the situation; its objective was Transylvania, which had been in Romanian hands since the Treaty of Trianon. In the summer of 1940, the territory was claimed from the Romanian Government, and was occupied by the Hungarians between 5-13 November.

BMW R-75 and Puch 350G motorcycles with sidecars belonging to the 3rd Motorcycle Company. In addition to tanks, motorcycles and bicycles were used by the Hungarian Army because of their off-road capability. Courtesy of Péter Mujzer.

Image of a row with four 35M Ansaldo tanks in an occupied town in the area of the Carpathians (Munkács) in 1939, where the movement of troops can be seen. After their first combats, the Hungarians decided to use the Ansaldo in secondary tasks. Courtesy of Károly Németh.

One of the virtues of the Ansaldo tank was its speed, which reached 43km/h on favourable terrain. A group of these tanks of the 1st battalion armoured cavalry advance towards the front, posing for the camera in March 1939 during the occupation of the Carpathians. The mechanical problems, the breakages and the lack of spare parts finally made them unusable. Courtesy of Károly Németh.

These Ansaldo tanks of the 2nd Reconnaissance Battalion somewhere in Transylvania in 1940, show why the national emblem was not popular among the crews. This emblem was a real target. It was not long after the cross's introduction before complaints began to be made. These came mainly from the crews, and more specifically from the drivers, of the Csabas, Toldis or Nimrods which already carried them. The reason for the complaints was that both the size and the brightness and the contrast of the cross made the crews feel as if they were right behind a target. This fact, together with the limited potential of Hungarian armoured vehicles, did little to help the crews' morale. It was this along with other factors, which motivated the Hungarian military authorities to change the badge to a more appropriate one. We can see that the first two tankettes have commander's observation cupola. Courtesy of Péter Mujzer.

A Csaba tank passes a Hungarian road control at the front. It was one of the first armoured vehicles of Hungarian manufacture that was in widespread use in Honved. In 1935 the engineers Michael Straussler and Manfred Weiss developed a 4 x 4 armoured reconnaissance vehicle that had a double driving position (one in the front and one in the rear). After several tests in which the Csaba held up well against other models of foreign manufacture, the army gave its approval for its serial production. Courtesy of Péter Mujzer.

Hungarian field artillery was already out of date at the beginning of hostilities, and nothing had improved by the time the war ended. After the Treaty of Trianon, the Army under the Regency of Admiral Miklós Horthy was limited to 35,000 men distributed in seven mixed brigades. The infantry units were at the level of before the First World War with no machine guns, only 70 light or medium mortars and only 105 10.5 cm howitzers for the heavy artillery. This was still the case, taking account of losses, by the end of the Second World War. Needless to say, the new kings of the battlefield such as aircraft and tanks were completely banned. Courtesy of Péter Mujzer.

The Toldi I could cope with muddy ground, but its flimsy armour was a problem. The first two appeared in February 1940 but the first order of twenty from the Ministry of Defence did not happen until June. Courtesy of Péter Mujzer.

A Rába Botond off-road truck pulling a trailer in 1941. The Rába 38M Botond was a Hungarian-made 1.5 ton all-terrain truck. It was used extensively during the war to carry both cargo and personnel. It was built on a Rába AFi truck chassis, in a configuration of 6x4. Courtesy of Péter Mujzer.

An Ansaldo tank tries to ford a river in Transylvania. The Ansaldo tanks had not been able to withstand the pressures that were asked of it. The mechanical problems, the breakages and the lack of spare parts gave huge trouble to this Italian-made unit. FORTEPAN MIHALYI BALAZS.

Cyclists in Transylvania played an important role in the whole campaign in this area but the mountainous terrain sometimes tested the fitness of the troops. In the summer of 1940, Transylvania was claimed by the Romanian government (which at that time was suffering a similar threat when claimed by the USSR in the Bucobina and Bessarabia regions) while the Hungarian army was waiting on the Romanian borders with the south-east of Hungary. The available vehicles were the obsolete Ansaldo, forty much more useful 38 M Toldis and thirteen M39 Csaba tanks, recently incorporated into the Hungarian Army the pride of the Hungarian arsenal. FORTEPAN 1594.

The Hungarian armoured vehicles receive a heartening welcome on 13 September 1940 in Kézdivásárhely, a town in western Transylvania. In the foreground, there is a Toldi I of the 2nd Reconnaissance Battalion with its tricolour badge. On 28 August 1940, the return of Transylvania to Hungary was finally confirmed. The conclusions of the campaign were very positive politically, but in regard to their armoured forces the same thing happened again as in the Ruthenian takeover, since both the Ansaldo and the Toldi and Csaba required urgent maintenance work to make them suitable for the wild Transylvanian countryside, though in the end, they were not needed for the campaign. FORTEPAN.

A column of 38M Botond in Transylvania. This Hungarian-made truck, together with the Krupp Protze and Ford trucks, were the most important transport and carrier vehicles in the Hungarian Army. The garlands on the front of the Botonds and the three tones of camouflage on the canvas of the second truck can be clearly seen. FORTEPAN KLENNER ALADAR.

Most of the Hungarian forces were not motorized, so the hypomobile option was selected in a multitude of cases. In the picture we can see a horse-drawn supply column during the march to the front line. They are on the left side of the road so as to leave the rest of the road to motorised vehicles. FORTEPAN KOKANY JENO.

Posters indicating the return of Transylvania to Hungary (Erdély in Hungarian). After Romania changed sides, the IV Hungarian Army was ordered to block the Russian/Romanian advance in the Arad and Lippa regions in the south Hungarian plain. VII Corps was added to IV Corps and redesignated the III Army, commanded by Lieutenant General Heszlényi. FORTEPAN DOBOCZI ZSOLT.

A 38M Toldi of the Light Tank Company belonging to the 1st Armoured Cavalry Battalion in Transylvania in 1940, bearing the white arching horseman emblem and the Mechanised branch sign. In the summer of 1940, Hungary claimed the territory from the Romanian government, positioning the army on the Romanian border in the southeast of Hungary. On this occasion, the armoured troops used the obsolete Ansaldo, as well as the much more useful 38 M Toldi (forty in total) and thirteen M39 Csaba tanks, recently incorporated into the Hungarian Army and the pride of the munitions industry in Hungary. The military occupation of Northern Transylvania was completed by 13 September. Courtesy of Péter Mujzer.

A Hungarian parade led by Ansaldo tanks in September 1940 in a town in Transylvania. This Italian-designed tank was developed in 1935 by Fiat and had an armament of two 8mm machine guns. Approximately 120 of these tanks served under the Hungarian flag (152 according to Becze). Despite the expectations placed on its use, it was soon clear that it was unsuitable in almost every way. They needed back-up from other vehicles and though one was adapted as a flamethrower, this was not performed widely. FORTEPAN 92486.

This photograph was taken in September 1940; a happy time for the Hungarian Army. A line up of 38M Toldi light tanks are resting in the town of Szásrégen, Transylvania, while a 39M Csaba armoured car passes by. These types of armoured vehicles were the spearhead of the Hungarian troops and the pride of the Hungarian armament industry. The 38M Toldi in the foreground bears a white lightning bolt on the right mudguard. FORTEPAN Varga Csaba dr.

The armoured vehicles that intervened in this 'peaceful' occupation consisted of the obsolete Ansaldo tankette, the 38M Toldi tanks (40 in total) and the armoured car M39 Csaba (13 in total), newly incorporated into the Hungarian army and the pride of native industry. Despite the fact that they did not participate in any combat, the difficulty of the terrain required urgent maintenance work on the Ansaldo, Toldi and Csaba.

In the spring of 1941, Hungary, as a result of their adherence to the Axis powers, took part in the German invasion of Yugoslavia. The attacking force comprised the III Hungarian Army (composed of the I, IV and V Corps and the Mobile Corps). It began its advance on 11 April in the Baranya region in the direction of

Little could be done in combat by the badly armed and worse armoured 35M Ansaldo tanks, which are seen here marching forward through the streets of a town. In 1934, Hungary began to increase its war potential with the acquisition of foreign material, specifically 150 Fiat-Ansaldo CV-33 tanks of Italian origin. Courtesy of Károly Németh.

A view of the front of a Toldi I with its 20mm gun which was clearly not enough for an armoured tank. It was based on the Swedish Landsverk L-60 tank, which underwent several modifications for production in Hungary such as ventilation, suspension, vision system or transmission. The most outstanding was the adoption of the 36M Solothurn 20mm antitank gun, which was accompanied by an 8mm coaxial machine gun (34/37 AM) and an R-5 radio. Courtesy of Károly Németh.

The Csaba tank, the pride of the Hungarian armaments industry, had very attractive lines, but inadequate armour. This tankette has a dark green camouflage and late style Hungarian badge. The main armament was the 36mm Solothurn 20mm gun and an 8mm machine gun, both located in a central turret. A second machine gun was positioned in the rear hatch for protection against aircraft protection but could also be used in reconnaissance by the crew, even on foot. Courtesy of Péter Mujzer.

This photo shows the Maltese Cross emblem on this Csaba tank, taken just before the war began. In the absence of any common national insignia for armoured troops, it was decided to hold a contest in July 1940 in which different units would put forward their own ideas for a new badge. The existing badge showed a Maltese Cross with different colours on the edge and inside a circle inside which varied in colour from one unit to the next. This badge was painted on all the vehicles that took part in the military operations in Transylvania, Yugoslavia and later Ukraine. Courtesy of Péter Mujzer.

Hungarian motorized troops wait their turn to cross a river. On the bridge, the ubiquitous Botond truck made in Hungary. Courtesy of Péter Mujzer.

A column of Csaba reconnaissance tankettes takes a short break before continuing its march. The tankettes belonged to the Armoured Tank Company of the 1st Reconnaissance Battalion. They were popular with their crews, but their defensive armour was very thin. The name 'Csaba' comes from the son of Attila the Hun who met the same fate as many Hungarian reconnaissance units. Courtesy of Péter Mujzer.

Hungarian cyclists get their orders before setting off on their mission at the front. On 29 June 1941, the Gyorshadtest had eight cyclist battalions: 6th, 7th, 9th, 10th, 11th, 12th, 13th and 14th distributed among their cavalry and motorized brigades. Troops from the 13th Cyclist Battalion formed in September 1940 on the Romanian-Hungarian border. Due to its ancestral enmity with Hungary, having Romania as a neighbour meant that throughout the Second World War, Hungarian troops monitored the border, even though they were both Axis allies. After Romania changed sides in September 1944, the Hungarian High Command had to outline a plan for the defence of Western Transylvania, which until then had only needed surveillance troops, but who now became front line soldiers. Courtesy of Péter Mujzer.

Cyclists try to make their way through to their destination. Such mobility as there was in the Hungarian army at the start of the Second World War was due to the army's cyclist units. Cyclists were used throughout the war, but they were most useful in the campaigns of 1938, 1939 and 1940. Courtesy of Péter Mujzer.

A Csaba tankette destroyed in July 1941 in Rogazna (Russia). Its flimsy armour left it weak against enemy fire even if the attack was of low calibre. It performed well in reconnaissance tasks although it paid dearly for its weak armour. By the end of 1941, more than 90 per cent of these vehicles had been destroyed. By then, its combat readiness was reduced and the few that were left were distributed among different units. Courtesy of Péter Mujzer.

Another Csaba tank put out of action by an enemy mine in Vojvodina in April 1941. The tarpaulin that covers it shows that it was due to be sent to the rear for service repairs. This tankette had four crew, a weight of 5,900kg, a shield of 13mm and a speed of 65km/h. Thanks to this, the vehicle was very popular with the crews, although very vulnerable to enemy fire. Courtesy of Péter Mujzer.

A Company of Csabas belonging to the 2nd Armoured Cavalry Battalion in Vojvodina in April 1941. In the front of the first Csaba we can see a bundle of logs ready to be used to try and make the muddy road more passable. Courtesy of Péter Mujzer.

A gathering of the 15th Cyclist Battalion where we can see an Ansaldo tank, as well as other anti-tank weapons and machine guns. The Cycling Battalions generally acted in support and reconnaissance missions and in addition to the soldiers with bicycles, they also had small armoured vehicles such as the Ansaldo tankettes or the 39M Csaba. Courtesy of Péter Mujzer.

A Csaba tank temporarily out of service after falling into a snow-filled ditch. FORTEPAN Ludovika.

the Danube. Only five days before, the bulk of the German troops had begun the attack on Yugoslavia. The Mobile Corps again contained the 38M Toldi and 39 Csaba that joined the outdated 35M Ansaldo.

The number of casualties in the Yugoslav campaign was quite low due to the weak resistance suffered by the Hungarians, so that the great limitations of the Hungarian armoured forces and, in general, all Hungarian armed forces were not realized.

The campaign in the USSR, 1941

Initially, Hungary did not take part in Operation Barbarossa on 22 June 1941 against the Soviet Union, but after the alleged Soviet bombardment of the Hungarian cities of Kassa and Munkacs on 26 June, war was declared with the USSR the next day.

On 27 June 1941, the Hungarian troops of the 'Carpathian' Group composed of the Mobile Corps (known as Gyorshadtest), the 1st Mountain Brigade and the 8th Border Brigade began to move towards Soviet territory from the eastern foothills of the Carpathians, before being integrated into the 17th German army. The Gyorshadtest was assigned to the area of Huzst-Marmarossziget-Borkut under the command of Major General Béla Dálnoki Miklós and had 75-80 per cent of its optimum potential: eighty-one 38m Toldi Is, sixty 35m Ansaldos and forty-eight 39 Csabas. Later fourteen Toldis, five Ansaldo tankettes and nine Csabas were brought in to replace vehicles that were out of action. the unit was able to act independently and on paper it was very powerful. In reality, it was really only comparable to a Soviet motorized Corps.

The Mobile Corps on 29 June 1941 was composed of: 1st Motorized Brigade (under Major General Jenö); 2nd Motorized Brigade (under Major General János Vörös); 1st Cavalry Brigade (under Major General Antal Vattay); and other small units.

Each of the two motorized brigades that were part of the Mobile Corps, had thirty-six 38m Toldi Is and sixteen 39 Csaba reconnaissance vehicles. The 1st Cavalry Brigade only had nine 38m Toldi Is and thirty-six 35M Ansaldos for its reconnaissance.

After taking the mountain passes of Pantyr and Tatár in the Carpathians the Gyorshadtest would take the lion's share of the advance to Galitzia in Ukrainian territory. The advance began very slowly because of the resistance of the Red Army. When the mountain paths were left behind the Gyorshadtest began to show its prowess as it advanced further into the vastness of the USSR. On 7 July, they crossed the Dniester, and were now under the command of the German Army Group South under Field Marshal von Rundstedt.

As part of the 17th German Army, the Gyorshadtest joined the march to Kiev. After this, it was assigned to the 1st German Panzer Group attacking the Stalin Line. The Hungarians destroyed a number of Soviet vehicles and captured at least 13 tanks and 12 artillery pieces, breaking the Russian defensive line.

The commander of the Toldi I poses for the camera in 1941. The three-tone octagonal emblem and a white eagle (turul) of a battalion of cavalry are clearly visible both on the hatch and on the side of the vehicle. The new battle tank was named 38M Toldi I (in honour of the fourteenth-century Hungarian warrior Miklos Toldi) and its production under licence was entrusted to the MÁVAG and Ganz factories. Courtesy of Károly Németh.

A Toldi I, recognizable by its antenna, participates in a parade after the first border fighting action in which the Hungarian army took part. The 38M Toldi I, although manufactured in Hungary, still had different parts that had to be acquired in Sweden and Germany, in spite of which it reached a total production of 80 units between the years 1940 and 1941. Courtesy of Károly Németh.

A T-26 put out of action by the Hungarians. During the advance on Russia in 1941, the Hungarian armour was a tough rival for the Russians. The Russians had in their armoury some obsolete models such as BT-2, BT-5, BT-7, T-26, T-37 and T-38, which although they had larger calibre guns than their Hungarian opponents, still lacked adequate shielding to withstand the 38M Toldi I 20mm guns. FORTEPAN BERKO PAL.

Two soldiers pose next to a 37M Hansa Lloyd half-track, which was normally required to haul artillery pieces. In 1937, Hungary bought 74 Hansa Lloyd 37M tractors from the German Government, better known by its German name of Sd.Kfz.II. This was a half-track tractor that saw a widespread use in the Second World War and carried eight soldiers, in addition to towing an artillery piece or a trailer. Courtesy of Péter Mujzer.

Part of the Hungarian mobile park was made up of sidecar bikes that provided speed and versatility, as well as a place to rest their crew. In this image, an officer tries to sleep on his CWS MIII Sokol 1000. The Sokol 1000 (also known as CWS MIII) was the heaviest Polish pre-war motorcycle manufactured by the PZInz works, for both civilian and military use. Its top speed was 100km/h. Among the most notable innovations was a soft sidecar mounting, which allowed for easier handling and greater off-road speed. Courtesy of Péter Mujzer.

Proof of the uselessness of the Hungarian light anti-tank guns is clearly seen here on an abandoned KV-1 along the Don River; the shell blocked by the thick armour. Hungarian armoured troops, had completely inadequate 40mm calibre guns which were unable to combat the Russian tanks such as the KV-1 or the T-34. FORTEPAN KONOK TAMAS ID.

Hungarian casualties amounted to six 38m Toldi Is destroyed and seven damaged, as well as three 39 Csabas. The Hungarian armoured forces proved to be tough opponents for the Red Army, especially because several of the Soviet armoured vehicles (BT-2, BT-5, BT-7, T-26, T-37 and T-38) were obsolete.

Between 22-29 July, the Gyorshadtest was involved in mopping up operations of the Soviet troops still positioned west of the Bug River; thirty-two Toldis and eighteen Ansaldos were lost. To compensate for these high numbers, replacements (fourteen 38 Toldi Is, nine 39 Csabas and five 35M Ansaldos) were sent from Hungary by rail on 27 July.

At the end of July, the Gyorshadtest was in the south-west of Uman, west of the Bug, working with German troops to surround important Soviet units, especially the 6th and 12th Armies, in the Uman pocket. On 8 August, the besieged Russians (about 100,000 men) surrendered unconditionally.

Later, the Gyorshadtest would participate in the offensive towards Mykolaiv, which fell on 17 August. After that, the unit was entrusted with taking positions on the right bank of the River Dnieper about 200km to the left of the 3rd Romanian Army. The Hungarian High Command began to doubt whether they could hold

Two Turán Is exercising in the training field before taken over for military purposes. They were still driven by factory workers. Under-armed and worse armoured, they were in no sense rivals of their Russian counterparts. Following the Huba modernisation programme of the Hungarian army, the total production of 40M Turáns (Turán I) reached 235 (285 according to Németh) tanks, manufactured by the Weiss Manfréd (70), Magyar Waggonyár (70), MÁVAG (50) industries and Ganz (45). Courtesy of Károly Németh.

this position for long. During the advance of the Gyorshadtest, maintenance or replacement of the lost vehicles did not take place. The problem was that the best Hungarian units had to be held back inside Hungary to prevent any type of attack from Romania. Despite the fact that both countries were fighting on the same side against the Russians, the age-old rivalry between them continued. Gradually, the different Hungarian units were sent home, the Gyorshadtest remaining active until 24 November.

After five months of intense fighting, the results were disastrous. It had been difficult to maintain vehicles and almost impossible to replace them. About 200 officers and 2,500 men were dead, 1,500 were missing in action and there were some 7,500 injured. The armoured vehicles were badly hit, losing all the Ansaldo tanks, 80 per cent of the Toldi I medium tanks and 90 per cent of the rest. On the positive side, the Hungarian army had captured more than 8,000 Russians and 65 guns, as well as 50 battle tanks.

After this Russian experience, the Hungarian High Command knew that expansion and improvement of the army was essential. This was called the 'HUBA II plan', a continuation of 'HUBA I' that took place before the war. Changes were already obvious before the end of 1941 but were not completed until 1942.

Chapter Three

Action in the Ukraine, 1942

At the start of 1942, the Hungarian involvement on the Eastern Front was limited to occupation in the rear; but Germany needed Hungarian support in the battles of the Eastern Front. After many negotiations, the Hungarian government offered the 2nd Army. This new unit had some 200,000 men under the command of Colonel General Gusztav Jany. It was composed of three Army Corps (6th, 7th and 9th Infantry Divisions), a fourth Corps (10th,

Impressive demonstration of Hungarian armour with a number of Pz 38 of the 1st Armoured Division and Nimrods of the 51st self-propelled Anti-Aircraft Battalion ready for action and on parade before their deployment to the front in April 1942. Hungary received 108 tanks of this model with a 37mm gun from Germany. It was the first attempt by the country to buy modern armoured materiel abroad. The main problem is that when they were received (in 1942) they were already obsolete, so they were not much use against the Soviet armour where they were under-armed and under-armoured. Courtesy of Károly Németh.

Hungarian troops clashing with the Russians in 1942. In the summer of that year, the Germans demanded the maximum effort from Hungary in the fighting on the Eastern Front. This involved virtually the entire Hungarian army. Faced with these demands, the Hungarians offered their 2nd Army as an alternative. Hitler accepted this and ordered the 2nd Hungarian Army to be relegated to a German Army Group. FORTEPAN Gráficas Lajos.

A 28M Pavesi with protective canvas cover, produced in Hungary under licence from the Italian Pavesi company. It carried a 15cm 31M howitzer in 1942. In order to transport the guns, as well as the Pavesi, the main mode of transport in the 1930s, Hungary also bought from Germany seventy-four copies of the Hansa Lloyd 37M tractor (better known by its German name of Sd.Kfz.11) in 1937. These were used as tractors for the 40mm Bofors anti-aircraft gun and the 105mm 37M light howitzers. FORTEPAN Konok Tamas ID.

12th and 13th Infantry Divisions) and the VII Corps (19th, 20th and 23rd Infantry Divisions), as well as the 1st Armoured Division and several independent units.

The Hungarian armoured forces had better armoured vehicles like the Panzer 38 (Pz 38 or Skoda 38 (t)), the Panzer I and IV F-1 and the light Toldi tanks.

The spearhead of the 1st Armoured Division was the 30th Armoured Regiment consisting of two battalions. Each battalion had a company of heavy tanks with eleven PZ IV F-1s, three PZ 38s and one 38M Toldi; and two medium tank companies each with twenty Pz 38s. In addition, there were several ambulance and command vehicles. Its total strength was one hundred and four Pz 38s, twenty-two Pz IV F-1s, six Toldis and six Pz Is. In addition to the 30th Armoured, we must highlight the presence of other vehicles such as the 40M Nimrod anti-aircraft armoured cars and the 39 Csaba armoured cars.

The 2nd Army was ordered to control a sector of the Don River, arriving on 7 July to its deployment zone of about 200km of the west bank. This left the armoured unit as the reserve of the 2nd Army. At that time, in the western sector of the river, the Russians still held three bridgeheads – Uryv, Korotyak and in Shchuche (Shchuchye), posing very serious problems for the Hungarians.

Miklós Horthy inspects the inside of a Pz IV F-1, marked with the Hungarian emblem at that time consisting of a green cross with white trim on a red octagon, used just after the Hungarian occupation of the Yugoslav territories in the spring of 1941. Its use coincides in part with that of the Maltese Cross and in many units the new badge was implemented while others still kept the old one. Courtesy of Károly Németh.

A Pz IV F-1 manoeuvring on a slope. This battle tank was the first which was really comparable to those used by the enemy. It was the first battle tank that the Hungarians possessed, capable of facing their Soviet opponents in equal conditions. With its short 75mm KwK 37 L/24 gun, the Germans considered it a medium tank, while the Hungarians considered it a heavy tank. Courtesy of Károly Németh.

The magnificent Hungarian-made Nimrod self-propelled anti-aircraft vehicle was one of the most valued in terms of its versatility. In 1942, these were part of the 51st self-propelled Anti-Aircraft Battalion which had three companies with six 40M Nimrods and 38M Toldi Is each. To these we must add three 38M Toldis and one 40M Nimrod of the Battalion HQ. Courtesy of Károly Németh.

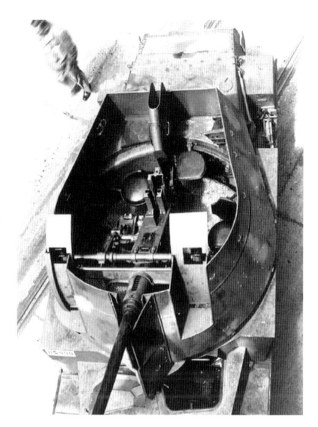

Top view of a 40M Nimrod. We can see clearly its open compartment with the crew four positions. A feature of the gun that it carried was its high fire rate – 120 rounds/minute with a speed of exit of the projectile of 881m/s. Its average armament load of armament was 160 shells. Courtesy of Károly Németh.

A BT 7 captured from Russians being shown to the public in 1942. During the invasion of Russia, a certain amount of Russian armour fell into Hungarian hands, still in good condition. However, they were not used for combat but as tractors. Among these were more than six BT-7s and T-26s as well as a possible six BA-6s that were captured between 1941 and 1942. FORTEPAN NAGY GYULA.

A KV-1 put out of action by the Hungarians in 1942. At the time of the invasion of the Soviet Union by Germany and its allies in the Second World War, the KVs were the best protected tanks, which together with the small calibre of the Hungarian anti-tank guns, made their destruction difficult and success rare. FORTEPAN KONOK TAMAS ID.

A proud Hungarian soldier poses with a 36M 40mm Bofors gun. This was the same one that used the 40M Nimrod and it was shown as a high-value fast-fire weapon against low-armoured targets and even with some success against vehicles with thicker armour at short distances. FORTEPAN 19259.

Several newly manufactured Nimrods rest in a military depot before being sent to their destination unit. In September 1940, Hungarian engineers realised that both the speed of the anti-aircraft gun and its recoil were too fast for the chassis it was mounted on and so it could cause serious malfunctions and even accidents. This forced them to discard that option and take the field gun, which in itself already posed the limitation of not being able to be incorporated into a turret with 360° rotation. To prevent this, it was embedded in the chassis with a lateral deviation of about 30° to the right and a little more to the left; as well as -10° and 30° in the vertical. It was proposed to equip it with about 50mm of armour and a semi-automatic loading system, but all this increased its cost and finally, in February 1942, the project was cancelled. FORTEPAN Lissák Tidavar.

This German-made semi-track Sdfkz 8 worked well as a heavy artillery tractor. It is believed that the Hungarian army also had some Sd.Kfz.7 of smaller tonnage than the Sd.Kfz.8 but there is no photographic evidence. In the photo here, a Sdfkz 8 is in action in Kerepes. Public domain.

The order of battle of the 1st Armoured Division at this time, was the following (according to Stenge and Cloutier):

30th Armoured Regiment.
30/I Armoured Battalion (with its companies 30/1, 30/2 and 30/3).
30/II Armoured Battalion (with its companies 30/4, 30/5 and 30/6).

1st Brigade of Motorized Rifles.
1st Motorized Rifle Battalion.
2nd Motorized Rifle Battalion.
3rd Motorized Rifle Battalion.

51st self-propelled Anti-Aircraft Battalion.
1st Motorized Signal Battalion.
1st Motorized medium howitzers Battalion.
5th Motorized medium howitzers Battalion.
2nd Anti-Aircraft Battalion.
1st Reconnaissance Battalion.
1st Sapper Company.
1st Traffic Control Company.
1st Motorized Supply Battalion.

During this period, there were various clashes over the bridgeheads in Uryv and Korotoyak.

First Battle of Uryv

On 18 July, the 7th Light Division supported by the 30/I Armoured Battalion, the 51st self-propelled Anti-Aircraft Battalion and the 1st Motorized Rifle Battalion began the attack against Soviet troops of the 24th Armoured Corps. This had more than 100 tanks among which were the powerful T-34/76 as well as T-60, KV-1 and M3 Stuart. In this attack, the Hungarians managed to put out of action twenty-one enemy armoured vehicles mainly thanks to the Pz IV. The 40m anti-aircraft Nimrod showed their usefulness against troops on the ground.

After the first day of fighting, the Hungarians had managed to dislodge the Russians from the bridgehead, but a Soviet counteroffensive followed immediately and the same night they retook their positions in Uryv driving the Hungarians back to their initial positions of 20 July.

Four Stuart light tanks were captured from the Russians; three were used as towing vehicles in the Armoured Division, while the fourth was sent to Hungary to be studied and tested.

A 40M Nimrod of the 51st self-propelled Anti-Aircraft Battalion participating in an anti-aircraft firing exercise. Later, it would prove its worth as an anti-aircraft and anti-tank weapon. The Nimrod is shown with three tone camouflage. Courtesy of Károly Németh.

An impressive view of the 40 mm gun of the Nimrod, which played an effective role in the Hungarian armoured units. In the first battle of Uryv the Nimrods showed that their versatility could also include ground combat. In fact, while the 30/I Company advanced, the Nimrods of the 3rd Company of the 51st self-propelled Anti-Aircraft Battalion, under the command of Captain Henkey-Hönig, served as support. Tanks of the 130th Soviet Armoured Brigade attacked from behind and outflanked the Pz 38. The Nimrods directed their guns against the Russians and blasted them from 500 or 600 metres away. Despite Russian superiority, luck favoured the Hungarians since one of the shots hit the sighting mechanism of the driver of a T-34 and destroyed it. Courtesy of Péter Mujzer.

Several Nimrods of the 51st self-propelled Anti-Aircraft Battalion in column are ready to shoot towards the side of the road in 1942; the guns are in high elevation and a range finder is visible. The first Battle of Uryv against the Russians made it clear that the only weapon that could guarantee success was the 75mm gun of the Pz IV, since the 37mm guns of the Pz 38 or the 40mm Nimrod, only managed to cause damage to the enemy at very short distances and then only if they were the oldest models in the Russian armoured arsenal. From the point of view of the preparation of the Hungarian armoured forces, they had clearly made good use of German training. One tactic they had learned was to wait for the crew of the T-34 to be blinded by the smoke of their own shots in order to be able to attack them from a more advantageous position in an encircling manoeuvre. FORTEPAN LUDOVIKA.

In the few moments of calm, it was necessary to attend to the care and maintenance of the vehicle, as we see here in the case of this 38M Raba Botond. Only a small part of the Honved was mechanized, so the maintenance of the vehicles was very important. The immensity of Russia, with notoriously bad communication channels was a great drawback in the Hungarian attempts. FORTEPAN LUDOVIKA.

An image of a Soviet KV-1 put out of action by the Hungarians. During the first battle of Uryv the Tank Company 30/III under the command of Captain Maklary struck the first blow against the Russian troops of the 24th Soviet Armoured Corps. This unit had more than 100 battle tanks, the powerful T-34/76 as well as T-60s, KV-1s and M3 Stuarts. In this attack, the Hungarians knocked out twenty-one enemy armoured vehicles, more than half of them using the Pz IV already proving their worth to the Hungarian army. Corporal Roszik destroyed four enemy tanks with his Pz IV. FORTEPAN KOKANY JENO.

A pair of Pz 38 cross a village after the first battle of Uryv on 22 July 1942. Despite representing an important step for the Hungarian troops, it was already obsolete at the time of acquiring it from the Germans. In 1942, the 30th Armoured Regiment of the 1st Armoured Division had, as follows: a heavy tank company with eleven Pz IV F-1s, three Pz 38s and one 38M Toldi; and two medium tank companies with twenty Pz 38s, three Pz 38s and two 38M Toldis modified as medical vehicles; three Pz 38s, two 38M Toldis and six control vehicles of the Regimental staff. There was also a reserve of six Pz 38s of the reserve battle tanks and two 38M Toldis. Courtesy of Péter Mujzer.

A fully built Bofors artillery piece in 1943. The Hungarian engineers had the good idea of fitting the Turán with a 40mm gun (specifically, it was 40mm L/45 with an output speed of 800m/s and a rate of fire of 16 shots/minute). This was a variant of the standard Hungarian anti-tank gun and it also shared ammunition with the Bofors gun also in the Hungarian arsenal. FORTEPAN LAKATOS MARIA.

First Battle of Korotoyak

Immediately after the end of the fighting at Uryv, the Hungarian Command decided to attack at Korotoyak. Again, the bulk of the attacking force was made up of the 1st Armoured Division reinforced by the now exhausted 12th Light Division. The Hungarians used one hundred and three Pz 38s, twenty Pz IVs, twelve 40 m Nimrods and seven 38 Toldis, as well as seven anti-tank cannons.

At six in the morning of 7 August, the armoured troops advanced to the Don, but the enemy resistance was fierce and they were stopped. The next day, an attack carried out by twenty Russian tanks was beaten back with the destruction of four of them. After this, Hungarian tanks were used as assault artillery in order to eliminate the Soviet resistance zones. This was partially completed by 9 August. The 1st Armoured Division lost thirty-eight Pz 38s, two Pz IVs and two 38M Toldis in this battle. After these engagements, the 1st Armoured Division was urgently needed in Uryv.

Second Battle of Uryv

On 10 August, the Hungarians 1st Armoured Division and the 13th Light Division began a new attack. This met with bad luck; the advance was stopped almost immediately and the Hungarians were forced to withdraw.

Second Battle of Korotoyak

During 8-9 August, a new Russian offensive was launched from the Korotoyak bridgehead. The only Hungarian armoured vehicles available were those belonging to 30/II Armoured Battalion, which managed to stop the Russian advance.

A Hungarian Pz 38 or T-38 or LT vz. 38 destroyed after the fighting. You can clearly see the licence plate of the vehicle. In the second battle of Uryv on 10 August 1942 the Hungarians led by the 1st Armoured Division and the 13th Light Division began a new attack, which was unsuccessful. Russian anti-tank firepower destroyed ten Pz 38s from 30/I Armoured Battalion. Courtesy of Károly Németh.

One of the first examples of the Pz IV F2 in the hands of the Hungarians. Compared to the F-I model, fire capacity was greatly improved. Pz IV F2 was the logical evolution of the F-I model, replacing its main weapon with the long 75mm KwK 40 L/43 gun that improved its anti-tank capability. About ten copies were deployed in the 1st Armoured Division in 1942. The tank in the picture wears the German grey camouflage. Courtesy of Károly Németh.

After the second battle of Uryv the 1st Armoured Division returned to Korotoyak, which led to a counter-offensive on 15 August. On this day, at least ten Soviet tanks were destroyed (T-60 and M3); and three days later, the front line was established. The only vehicles available after the second battle of Korotoyak were fifty-five Pz 38s, and fifteen Pz IVs. We must not forget the action of the 51st self-propelled Anti-Aircraft Battalion, since they shot down approximately 40 enemy aircraft (of the total of 63 shot down by the 1st Armoured Division's different units).

After this action, the Hungarians were finally withdrawn from Korotoyak, their positions taken over by the 336th German Division. This managed to destroy the enemy bridgehead at the beginning of September. This had repercussions, since the Russians decided to concentrate their forces in the Uryv bridgehead.

The exhausted First Armoured Division with four Pz IV F-2s, were reinforced by the Germans by the end of August. By 1 September the Division had eighty-five Pz 38s, twenty-two Pz IVs (F-1 and F-2) and five 38M Toldis thanks to support from the Germans.

Third Battle of Uryv

On 9 September, a new German-Hungarian offensive was launched against the Uryv bridgehead, the 1st Armoured Division leading the way. In this clash,

The Pz IV FI together with the Pz III M were the tip of the Hungarian spear in 1942. One of the Pz IV FIs received by the Hungarians from Germany, waits here in its barracks (Esztergom-Szentistvánváros). Twenty units of the Pz III Ms 50mm gun German tank were received by Hungary. They were distributed equally between the 1st and the 2nd Armoured Divisions. The small number of units received did not change the balance on the Hungarian side against the Russians. FORTEPAN 140945 Miklós Lajos.

several combat tanks – Pz IV F-1 and PZ 38 – were lost. On the 11th, thanks to great effort on behalf of Hungarians and Germans, Stotozhevoye was taken. At the end of the next day, they were only had four Pz IVs and twenty-two Pz 38s. A day later, these managed to destroy eight T-34 tanks and damage two KV-1s during a new Russian offensive. On the 16th, a new Russian attack was halted, which brought the third battle of Uryv to an end. The overall result was that the bridgehead could not be retaken and the casualties had been so great that the Hungarian armour was not fit for further combat. Because the 1st Armoured Division only had at this time two Pz IV F-1s and twelve Pz-38s, it was taken out of the front line.

To make up for Hungarian casualties, the Germans agreed to deliver ten Pz IV F-2s, ten Pz III Ms and possibly between four and eight Pz II Fs in October. In December, ten StuG III Ns with German crews were placed under the command of the Hungarians.

Despite the arrival of foreign armoured vehicles, the Hungarian munitions industry already began to work on new units that in a few months would be

Several Hungarian tanks, with two Pz IIs in the foreground, possibly waiting to be checked for early start-up. It was a completely obsolete armoured vehicle, but it proved useful as a reconnaissance tank. It was not often used in action. Courtesy of Károly Németh.

A column of Pz IV F-1s of the Heavy Tank Company of the Hungarian Tank Battalion advances through Russian-held territory during the campaign of 1942. By this time, the Hungarian armoured forces had improved, mainly thanks to the acquisition of materiel from the German arsenals such as the Panzer 38 or the Panzer I and IV F-1, possibly including some D models, together with the national Toldi light tanks, the Turán being not yet available. Courtesy of Péter Mujzer.

serving in the front at Turan or Zrínyi and that would lift the fighting potential of the Magyar Királyi Honvédség (land forces of the Kingdom of Hungary).

At the end of November, the Red Army began its offensive against the southern flank of the Axis troops near Stalingrad, by attacking the lines of Italians and Romanians. The Hungarian positions were somewhat further north. This attack forced the Germans to send reinforcements from other areas.

Because of the way in which the Hungarians had suffered fighting in Russia, the Hungarian High Command, realising the weakness of their armoured forces, decided to carry out the third part of the Huba Plan, 'HUBA III'. The idea was to carry this out throughout 1943 and after obtaining better, more modern and effective material, would put the Hungarian Armoured units in a far stronger position.

An image of the only prototype that was made of the Zrínyi I armed with a 75mm gun in the military depot of Tüzérszertár. Had Hungarian 44M Zrínyi I been manufactured, this powerful tank destroyer would undoubtedly have been a serious rival to the Russian armour and in some ways would have tipped the balance of the fighting towards the Hungarians. Behind this one can see a Zrínyi II with its 105 mm Howitzer. Courtesy of Károly Németh.

A side image of a Zrínyi II where we can clearly see the emblem with the white cross on black square that the Hungarian armoured troops used for most of the war. This new badge had to be painted in three different sizes depending on which part of the vehicle it was used on, eg the sides or engine parts. Oddly, it was not painted on the armoured turrets; and it was forbidden to be carried on the front of the vehicles, because it was considered as a target for the driver's position. Courtesy of Károly Németh.

A Mercedes Benz L 3000 and a T-34/76 captured in 1942. This Russian tank was the main obstacle to the Hungarian armoured forces and was difficult to destroy. The short 75mm gun developed by the MÁVAG, was clearly insufficiently powerful to pierce the frontal armour of a T-34 except practically at point-blank range. The T-34s were more vulnerable to the German made Pz-IV, Panzers and Tigers. FORTEPAN 12638.

Photograph showing a Toldi II with a pair of Toldi Is behind, showing the emblem that the Hungarian armed forces began using in 1942. On 16 November, the previous tricolour badge was replaced by a new one which would be used by all vehicles of the Hungarian armoured forces. This new unifying insignia was the same as the one that was being used in the Hungarian Air Force and consisted of a white cross on a black square. FORTEPAN.

A command Toldi followed by a Toldi adapted to provide first aid cover cross a ford of a river during the campaign of 1942. Nine Toldi Is were modified to provide health care in the first line of fire; in this case they maintained their functional gun although with less ammunition. These vehicles were modified in 1942 and they were called 43M Toldi Egészségügyis (doctors). According to Becze, four vehicles were adapted in 1942 and nine between 1943 and 1944. They were able to carry two stretchers and had enlarged doors to facilitate access. They were incorporated into the 2nd Army, where they acted in the front line. Courtesy of Péter Mujzer.

Several Hungarian soldiers look over a Russian T-28 tank that they have put out of action in 1942. The T-28 was an infantry supporting tank, designed to cross fortified lines. Despite its 76.2mm gun, its 11-30mm armour was not enough to withstand the 20mm guns of the 38M Toldi I. Visible in the background is a Hungarian support vehicle that allowed good speed to the Hungarians provided the road was in good condition. FORTEPAN 20345.

Chapter Four

Reorganization After the Storm, 1943

O n 2 January, the 1st Armoured Division became part of the Cramer Group, the reserve unit of Army Group B. This consisted of the 26th and 168th German Divisions, with 190 field pieces and 700 armoured vehicles. Four days later, the Hungarians received five Marder IIs. These tank hunters were integrated into a new unit, the 1st Independent Tank Hunter Company.

One of the few Marder IIs given to Hungary as a loan. Its formidable firepower represented an important improvement in Hungarian armour. On 6 January 1943, the Hungarians were lent five Marder II tank destroyers under the command of Captain Zergényi, which would be manned by the 51st self-propelled Anti-Aircraft Battalion and the 30th Armoured Regiment. Courtesy of Károly Németh.

The Hungarian Marder II carried the original German emblem. Here we see one of these tank destroyers in the ceremony for the withdrawal of the 2nd Hungarian Army from the operational area. This German tank destroyer was based on the chassis of the Pz II with various models A/B/C/F. With its powerful 75mm gun, even though few vehicles were leased to Hungary by Germany, it was one of the most impressive weapons used against the Russians. FORTEPAN 131348 Marics Zoltán.

The only example of the Toldi PaK 40 L/48 tank destroyer. It had a number of drawbacks so it never went into production. The Institute of Hungarian Military Technology borrowed several German Marders which had proved invaluable and carried out tests and a detailed study of them. The idea was to build a Hungarian Marder, a tank destroyer based on the Toldi chassis, but with the open structure housing a non-rotating German gun PaK 40 of 75mm L/48. It was Ganz's responsibility to develop a prototype from a damaged Toldi I in autumn 1943. Courtesy of Károly Németh.

The next day, they took possession of sixteen Pz IVs (eight short barrelled and eight long barrelled), forty-one Pz 38s, two 38M Toldi Is, five Marders, some 40M Nimrods and nine Pz III Ms.

But the situation was about to change. On 12 January there was a strong Russian attack against the front held by the rather weakened Hungarian troops from Uryv, Schutschye and Kantemirovka.

The Moskalenko 40th Soviet Army, with one Guards Rifle Division, four Rifle Divisions, one Rifle Brigade and three Tank Brigades launched an assault from the Uryv bridgehead. The Tank Brigades had 164 battle tanks that included thirty-three KV-1s and fifty-eight T-34s, as well as tank destroyers and rocket launchers.

The 18th Soviet Rifle Corps broke out from the Schutschye bridgehead with three Rifle Divisions, one Rifle Brigade and two Tank Brigades which had up to 150 tanks that included one KV-1 and fifty-six T-34s as well as the usual artillery backup.

The 3rd Soviet Armoured Army launched an attack from the Kantemirovka area with 425 battle tanks, including 29 KV-1s and 221 T-34s.

There was total confusion as many units lacked proper armament and ammunition, so Hungarian veterans held on by sheer willpower as all hell broke loose.

The 1st Armoured Division counter-attacked on 16 January having received orders to try to seal the gaps in the defensive line and to support the withdrawal of the Hungarian troops.

View of a 43M Lehel transport armoured vehicle, based on the Nimród chassis. Had it been manufactured in adequate quantities, it would have been a vital element in the Hungarian war effort. In 1942, there was a proposed adaptation of the 40m Nimród, in which the turret would be eliminated and adapted to transport troops. Two versions of the new vehicle were developed: the Lehel A (transport of troops with capacity of 8 men, protected by a machine gun) and the Lehel S (medical transport with capacity to carry four stretchers). Although the complete design was presented in 1943, the wartime situation was such that it was never developed. Courtesy of Károly Németh.

The next day, the 1st Armoured Division launched a counter-attack with eight PZ IIIs and four Pz IVs towards Dolschik-Ostrogosshk destroying a column of Russian vehicles. They lost a lot of materiel that had to be left behind because of a lack of fuel and mechanical problems. The Pz 38s were totally useless with the snow so deep and the temperatures so extreme. 30/I Battalion had to blow up at least seventeen Pz 38s, two Pz IVs and other vehicles because they could not take them with them during the retreat.

On 18 January, the Armoured Division was to attack and retake Alekseyevka supported by the 559th German Tank Hunter detachment that was attached to it. After two and a half hours, the city was captured, but the next day abandoned after a new Russian attack. By 27 January, the 2nd Hungarian Army was almost annihilated.

The last important action took place on 7 February. Two days later, the Armoured Division crossed the River Donets, reaching Kharkiv and pulling out of the front line. At this time, the only armoured vehicles left to the Hungarian unit were two Marders.

In just eight days since the start of the offensive, the Russians had knocked out the last defensive positions of the exhausted Hungarian forces in villages

This is the only known image of the Hungarian 'Marder'. Despite its non-rotating 75 mm L/48 PaK 40 gun, based on a Toldi I, it was poorly shielded. The Ganz Works had developed this prototype in the autumn of 1943 from a Toldi I that was in repair. This substitute of the Marder had several drawbacks that led to it never going into mass production: its limited armour only resistant to rifle fire; the weakness of the cushioning system of Toldi I; its excessive height and narrow profile that made it unstable, and above all that the Hungarian industry had focused on the Turán and Zrínyi models. Courtesy of Károly Németh.

The first prototype of the Zrínyi II was made of steel. and was tested on 12 December 1942, to go into mass production on 20 January 20, 1943. The Zrínyi II (40/43M Zrinyi II) reached 43km/h on the road and carried a 105mm (40/43M L/20.5) howitzer, a version of the 105mm 40M field howitzer. The name Zrínyi is in honour of Nikolaus Graf Zrínyi, a national hero who died in the battle of Szigetvár against the Turks in 1566. Courtesy of Péter Mujzer.

Several Turán II battle tanks at a military depot waiting to be sent to their destinations; a photograph probably taken in 1943. The next tank to be made in Hungary after the Turán was the 44M TAS. Based on the German Panzer, the TAS had a 75mm gun (the German KwK 42L/70) and two 8mm machine guns and its frontal armour would be around 100-120mm thick. Its maximum speed by road was 48km/h and the crew would be five men, but only one prototype was built in March 1944 with none further being made, due mainly to the partial destruction of the Weiss factory by the Americans on 27 July 1944. FORTEPAN Lissák Tidavar.

like Novo Charkovka, Novo Postoialovka, Kopani, Valuiki or Podgornoye, from which only a few thousand men escaped.

1943 had begun disastrously for the Hungarians, who lost most of their troops and equipment during the Russian offensive. The losses were 107 tanks (22 Pz IVs, ten Pz IIIs, 64 Pz 38s, 11 Toldis), 3 Marder IIs, 15 Nimrods, 10 Csabas, 1,030 motor vehicles (681 trucks, 114 cars, 235 motorcycles), 17 10.5 cm artillery guns, 20 anti-tank guns and eight anti-aircraft guns, as well as a lot of smaller weapons. Despite this, the courage of Hungarian soldiers led them to receive more than 3,000 decorations for the bloody action between 1942 and 1943.

Armoured Vehicles on the Home Front

We must not forget the Hungarian troops that were in the rear, doing their job, maintaining the tank depots. In 1942 they were made up of the Independent Tank Squadrons (101st and 102nd), which took part in supporting the anti-partisan activities of the Hungarians in Ukrainian territory.

French tanks like this Somua S-35 of the 101st Independent Armoured Company cleverly camouflaged in a Polish village in 1943, were used by second-line units in anti-partisan tasks; due to their age they were not really suitable to be in the front line. Only two units of this French tank armed with a 47mm gun were added to the Hungarian arsenal. Both vehicles were used in anti-partisan work in Ukraine-Poland due to their very limited use when confronting the Russian tanks. In this image, we see a tank of the 101st independent squadron in a Polish town in mid-1943. Courtesy of Károly Németh.

Several French-made Hotchkiss H-39 tanks positioned next to anti-aircraft guns in second-line positions. All these vehicles were lost in the performance of anti-partisan tasks. Some units of this tank ended up being part of the Hungarian army. They arrived from Germany where they had been taken after the conquest of France. Their low combat capacity relegated them to anti-partisan tasks. Courtesy of Károly Németh.

The 101st had received looted combat tanks from France, two Somua S-35s acting as command vehicles and fifteen Hotchkiss H-35/h-39s.

The 102nd used Hungarian- made vehicles. The French tanks were gradually lost in the period between 1942-1944, either by attacks of partisans or by regular Russian troops and in some cases having to be destroyed by their own crews so as not to let them fall into enemy hands.

Chapter Five

Defending Hungary, 1944

After the 1st Armoured Division was almost destroyed on the Eastern Front in 1943, the task of rebuilding it began in the following year. A new armoured training unit was set up that would become the 2nd Armoured Division. The beginning of the year was easy for Hungary; the second half was hell.

After the Stalingrad disaster in February 1943, the demoralized Hungarian troops reconsidered their alliance with Germany. The German High Command did not approve of the fact that the Hungarians appeared to be badly led and

What became obvious was that armoured vehicles made in Hungary were no match for their Russian equivalents. The level of maintenance was minimal, and spare parts almost impossible to obtain. For this reason, the German High Command agreed on 4 May 1944 to re-equip with German vehicles. The training of Hungarian crews was carried out by the Germans. Here we see a Pz VI in the foreground; a StuG III and a Pz IV H are seen in the background. Courtesy of Károly Németh.

A new Hungarian crew listens avidly to the German instructors on the tower of a Tiger. The Hungarians should have received the new Schwere Panzer-Abteilung 509 Tigers, but contrary to orders, they received the Schwere Panzer-Abteilung 503 model. Training took place between May and June 1944 in Nadvorna, which unbeknownst to the Hungarians, had already become the Russians' next target. Courtesy of Károly Németh.

A propaganda poster of 1944 promoting Szálasi and his Arrow Cross party (Nyilaskeresztes Párt - Hungarista Mozgalom). This was a fascist, anti-Semitic and pro-German party, similar to the Nazis. It was led by Ferenc Szálasi, who ruled Hungary with German support between October 15, 1944 and March 28, 1945. The next day, the Government of Szálasi left Hungary, continuing its activity in Germany until arrested by the American army. FORTEPAN Lissák Tidavar 1944.

the whole situation finally led to the Germans occupying part of Hungary on 19 March 1944. This was Operation Margarethe. German troops from neighbouring Austria-Croatia entered Hungary peacefully, going no further than the River Tisza where the 1st Hungarian Army was deployed at that time. From this German occupied zone, Hungary was able to remobilize its troops, calling into service the 1st, 2nd and 3rd Armies, with the 1st and 2nd Armoured Divisions attached to them.

Hungarians in Poland

One unit that we have not talked about is the 1st Cavalry Division, mobilized on 29 April 1944 (the 26th according to Bernad) and sent to the front. The plan was to subordinate the unit to the 1st Hungarian Army in the Carpathians and to position it on the left wing. The Germans rejected this idea and the hussars were sent instead to the Pripet marshes, south of Belarus and to the northwest of the Ukraine. There they constituted the reserve of the German 2nd Army.

The 1st Cavalry Division participated in anti-partisan operations along railway lines, but once Operation Bagration was underway, it become a front line unit. The unit's 1st Battalion had a heavy tank company, three medium tanks companies

A Turán I advances through a combat zone. On the side of the road, Hungarian troops are seen taking a break. The Turán I entered service on 28 November 1941, being officially named 40.M Turán közepes harckocsi (middle tank) and colloquially Turán I or Turán 40. It was called Turán in homage to the Hungarian ancestral homeland in Central Asia. Courtesy of Károly Németh.

A prototype of the Turán I performs an exercise to demonstrate its cross-country capabilities. The first Turán prototype was produced by Manfréd Weiss on 8 July 1941. Due to some problems in suspension and transmission, mass production was delayed until the beginning of 1942. Despite the great leap for the Hungarian armaments industry, it was not really up to the standard needed by the time of the Second World War. Courtesy of Károly Németh.

Troops of Hungarian cavalry on reconnaissance. The 1st Cavalry Division was mobilized on 29 April 1944 and sent to the front. The plan was to subordinate it to the 1st Army in the Carpathians and position it on the left wing, but the Germans rejected this idea and the hussars were sent to other units, specifically the Pripet marshes, south of Belarus and northwest of Ukraine. There they made up the Reserve of the 2nd German Army with the title of 2nd Corps of Hungarian Reserve Corps. They reached Pinsk on 20 June and at Luninets the next day. FORTEPAN KOKANY JENO.

A maintenance workshop where several Turán tanks were built in 1942. Following the Huba program of the army's modernization, the total production of 40M Turán (Turán I) was 235 tanks. Seventy of them were manufactured by Weiss Manfréd, seventy by Magyar Waggonyár, fifty by Mávak industries and forty-five by Ganz. Oddly, the parts of the Turáns coming from the different manufacturers, were not exactly the same. FORTEPAN Lissák Tidavar.

A magnificent image of a Turán I armed with a 40mm gun. Badly armoured and poorly armed, it never matched rivals like the T-34 or the KV-1. This led, in May 1943, to the 41M Turán II with certain improvements including a short 75 mm gun developed by MÁVAG. This was clearly insufficient to reach the same standard as the Russian tanks since its low velocity projectile could not puncture the T-34's front shield, except at point-blank range. So the 75mm, based on the 76.6mm Böhler, recalibrated by the Bofors, was not much more effective than the 40mm Turán I. FORTEPAN Lissák Tidavar.

and one command company. In total they had twenty-five 38M Toldis, fifty-four 40M Turán 40s and eleven 41M Turán 75s. Other sources say that it comprised sixty-five medium, eleven heavy, five Toldis and three Pz 38s. The 1st Cavalry Division comprised the 15th Cyclist Battalion, which had a platoon with four 40M Nimrods, and the 3rd Reconnaissance Battalion with two companies of armoured vehicles, each with thirteen 39M Csabas.

The Russian offensive under Operation Bagration overwhelmed the front line of Army Group Centre, creating a large gap. Despite the enemy's superiority, the 1st Cavalry Division was given the task of plugging the gap. After leaving the Kletsk pocket and until 25 July, the Division was fighting a rear-guard action back to the Vistula River. During this withdrawal, most of the Division's armoured vehicles were lost. In fact, the 1st Cavalry Battalion lost all its battle tanks (84 in total) and the 3rd Reconnaissance Battalion only had six Csabas from the twenty-three that it had originally. Until 15 July, various units lost between 30-40 per cent of their original strength.

From August 1944, the 1st Cavalry Division was reorganized and received equipment, mainly anti-tank guns and anti-tank light weapons, from Germany. Only the 2nd cavalry remained completely on horseback, while the 3rd and 4th had an infantry battalion and a mounted battalion. The Division also received ten Hetzer tank destroyers, the first vehicles of this type in Hungary.

One of the few photographs where we can see a Hetzer tank destroyer with Hungarian insignia. It isn't clear just how many of these units were made but the number is somewhere between 75-150, used in the last years of the war. Interestingly, the first units of this vehicle supplied by the Germans went to the 1st Cavalry Division that was in Poland in August 1944. Courtesy of Károly Németh.

A Hetzer captured by the Russians who have put their identifying marks on it. The Germans had to reinforce the diminishing number of Hungarian armoured vehicles by providing 130 of these versatile light tank destroyers between 1944-45. With the 75mm L/48 gun and the 7.92mm machine gun, the Hetzer fought in the last battles in defence of Hungary before being finally overwhelmed by Russian troops. Courtesy of Károly Németh.

The 1st Cavalry Division operations in Poland ended in September 1944. They were sent back to Hungary to be reinforced with troops but no more armoured vehicles.

Fighting for Galicia

Because of the dazzling Russian advance already in western Ukraine, in the spring of 1944 the 1st Hungarian Army moved from the Carpathians to Galicia to stabilize the situation between North and South German Armies in the Ukraine. This held a line between Kolomyia, Otynia and Stanislavov (Ivano-Frankivsk).

The 2nd Armoured Division of the 1st Army, the most powerful unit within the entire Hungarian Army, was mobilized on March 13. All the armoured vehicles of the 2nd Armoured were made in Hungary: the 40M and 41 Turán, 40M Nimrod, 39M Csaba and 38M Toldi. The 2nd Armoured Division had 120 Turán medium combat tanks, 55 Turán heavy combat tanks, 84 Toldi light tanks (47 of them were armed with cannons of 40 mm), 42 Nimrod anti-

A Turán tank crossing a field bridge. This tank was under-gunned and under-armoured, so the Hungarian munitions industry tried to improve it by means of the Turán III. The Turán III would have represented an important step forward in Hungarian manufacture but was still inferior to anything the Russians already had in service. The maximum shielding of the Turán was 50 mm at the front, reaching at 60 in the last models. In other parts of the tank they varied between 8-25 mm in horizontal parts and 25-40 mm in the vertical ones. In the case of Turán III, the front plates would have reached 80 mm thick and the lateral skirts of 8 mm became standard. FORTEPAN 130014 Lázár György.

aircrafts and 14 Csabas. However, the Division did not have maintenance units to keep the tanks in serviceable condition.

Between 5 and 11 April 1944, the 2nd Armoured Division, under the command of Colonel Osztovics, arrived in Stryi. From there they had to travel between

A Toldi IIAK with side skirts that increased its durability in combat missions, although it was never good at withstanding the Russian anti-tank guns. Although the incorporation of armoured side skirts was interesting, they were ineffective against the firepower of the Soviet tanks and added an extra weight of 500kg to the vehicle, so it was never manufactured in useful numbers. Courtesy of Károly Németh.

Another image of the command Turán from which only this prototype was made in 1943. The Hungarians tried to copy the same type of command vehicle that the Germans had been using for years. The tank in the picture wears the three tones camouflage and the white cross over black square insignia, with no unit insignia painted. Courtesy of Károly Németh.

A column of Nimrods parades through a town with its guns at maximum height. During combat, despite its intended use against aircraft and light armour, it could be very effective when penetrating 46mm armour at 100m and 30 mm at 1,000m. The Nimrod had relatively thin armour (28mm in the turret and 13mm in the vertical plates) and the open turret gave it a high shape. Courtesy of Károly Németh.

Two Nimrods participating in an anti-aircraft firing exercise in Galicia. Some infantrymen are relaxed and 'enjoying' them. The production of this superb armoured vehicle started immediately, with 135 made between 1940 and 1943. The 40M Nimrod was a real revolution in the world of armoured vehicles, since its 40mm open turret gun (36M Bofors L/60), meant that it could be used against both aircraft and tanks. Courtesy of Károly Németh.

The prototype of a Nimrod with a high explosive 42aM muzzleloader. They tried to improve the firepower of the Nimrod, equipping them with the 42M Kerngranate that allowed them to shoot high explosive anti-tank grenades with a hollow charge of 15 cm. It was a muzzle-loading weapon similar to the operation of firing a grenade from a rifle. This prototype did not go into production. Courtesy of Károly Németh.

Another image of an anti-aircraft fire exercise involving two Nimrods of the 51st Anti-Aircraft Battalion and one 36M Bofors Anti-Aircraft gun, all using the same 40 mm gun. As the war went on and Russian armour improved, the 40M Nimrod continued to prove its worth against enemy light vehicles, infantry or cavalry. Courtesy of Károly Németh.

Two Turán IIs captured by the Soviets being prepared for transport to the USSR by train after capture. The 41M Turán II was also known as Turán 75 rövid (short), Nehéz Turán (heavy Turán) or simply T-75. There were 139 Turán IIs made between 1943 and 1944 (according to Németh there were between 182-185 cars, including some Turán Is, that were improved to the level of Turán II). By courtesy of Károly Németh.

Several Hungarian Engineers watch a Turán II fording a river, during a pause in the fighting in Galicia in 1944. The severe damage suffered by the 2nd Hungarian Armoured Division led to the decision to withdraw it from the frontline to be reorganized in Huszt. On 9 August the Division had fourteen Toldis, forty Turán-40s, fourteen Turán-75s, one Panzer III, one StuG III G and nine Panzer IV Hs. Three tough Tiger tanks had also survived, but they were damaged and had to be repaired later. Courtesy of Károly Németh.

250 and 300km under their own steam to the front, advancing in muddy terrain on snow-covered roads. Once at the front, the Division was divided into two combat groups deployed in a sector of about 60-70km wide.

Another unit also assigned to the 1st Hungarian Army was the 1st Assault Gun Battalion under the command of Captain Barankay (a veteran from 1942 campaigns). The main materiel was the brand new assault howitzer made by the Hungarian manufacturer Zrínyi. The 2nd and 3rd batteries of the Battalion left for the front on 12 April, arriving four days later.

The 2nd Armoured's first mission took place between 17-19 April alongside German troops. They launched an attack from Solotvyn to Nadvorna, Deliatyn and Kolomyia, with support from German combat armour, fifteen Marder from 615th Tank Hunter Battalion, seven Pz IVs and nine Tigers from 503rd Panzer Battalion. Nadvorna and Deliatyn were captured on 18 April after intense fighting which allowed two bridgeheads to be established on the banks of River Bistrica. The 1st Army had achieved its goal of linking the two German Army Groups, although the fighting exposed the weaknesses of the Turáns, because a T-34 could destroy them from between 1500-2000m away. The Turán only had a range of 600m with a 75 mm cannon or 400m in the case of a 40 mm cannon.

For this reason, the German High command agreed on 4 May to partially reequip the 2nd Armoured with German materiel. Between 6 and 14 May, twelve Pz IV Hs, ten Pz VI E Tigers, and ten StuG III Gs were delivered to Nadvorna. 3/I Battalion was given German equipment while 3/II Battalion was given the Hungarian Turáns.

The remains of Captain Barankay of the 1st Assault Gun Battalion rest on a Zrínyi II, watched over by his honour guard, being buried with full honours in Stanislau. Captain Barankay was killed in an air strike on 13 July in the town of Targowica (still within his own lines) while directing his vehicles towards Ottynia. Courtesy of Károly Németh.

A T-34/76 captured by the Hungarians, painted in the national colours (red, white and green) on the turret. Only very rarely were they used in combat against their original owners. T-34 guns were able to penetrate any Hungarian-made tank's armour at normal combat ranges. It is possible that there were some T-34/85 units among those captured by the Hungarian forces. Courtesy of Károly Németh.

A Turán I going up an embankment during manoeuvres. 279 were made between 1942 and 1944. It had a crew of five, a weight of 18.2 tons and a speed of 47 km/h. Courtesy of Károly Németh.

Several Hungarian soldiers pose on a Pz IV H with side skirts. Early in the war, Germany had to reinforce the armoured capacity of its allies, with 72 units being received by the Hungarians in 1944. These tanks had the powerful anti-tank gun KwK 40 L/48 of 75mm, giving 80 mm of frontal protection. The Pz IV H became the core of Hungarian armoured power. Courtesy of Károly Németh.

After re-equipping, the Battalion 3/I had four companies, the 1st with eleven Pz IV Hs, the 2nd with six Tigers, the 3rd with six Tigers and the 4th with nine StuG IIIs. One of the companies that had the mighty Tigers was commanded by 1st Lieutenant Ervin Tarczay and the other one by Captain János Vetress. Surplus vehicles left by various companies were delivered to the Division's 3/II Battalion eventually. In addition to the ten Tigers received, the Germans provided three more. A training unit was created for the new German materiel, possessing one Tiger, one Pz IV H and one StuG III.

Two Pz IV Hs are seen here waiting in a concentration zone. It is noteworthy that they show the German insignia instead of the Hungarian, which was relatively frequent from 1944. The thirty-two Pz IVs received by the Hungarians between the months of May and August of 1944 would be of the Pz IVG model; from September 1944 they were an iteration of Pz IVH. As a curiosity the last delivery of these vehicles to the Hungarians took place as late as March 1945, when several were delivered. Courtesy of Károly Németh.

A poor quality but extremely important image of a StuG III of the 7th Assault Gun Battalion in action. There were 50 StuG IIIs delivered to Hungary (according to Károly Németh, the number would reach up to 60, of which 20 of them would only be controlled temporarily by the Hungarians), which meant that in 1944 there were 40 units with the 7th Assault Gun Battalion of the 1st Division Hungarian armoured unit, as well as others that served in the 2nd Armoured Division. Courtesy of Károly Németh.

Close-up of First Lieutenant Ervin Tarczay (left), the most recognized ace of the Hungarian armoured forces in the Second World War. Although he excelled in the combats commanded by his Tiger, in the first days of August 1944 the Tiger was out of service so he had to use a Panzer and later in January 1945 he was in command of a Pz IV H, with which he also showed his combat expertise. This national hero and ace of the Hungarian armour was killed on 18 March 1945, after destroying more than 15 enemy battle tanks and at least a dozen anti-tank guns. Courtesy of Károly Németh.

Ervin Tarczay poses on his Pz VI Tiger in this front view of it taken in June 1944. He achieved many of his victories in in this vehicle. In one of the actions of that summer in the vicinity of Saturnia, he managed, supported by two Tigers, to destroy 14 enemy armoured vehicles (mainly T-34s) in an hour without suffering any casualty. Courtesy of Károly Németh.

Tarczay in his Pz VI Tiger. Only Hungary, among all the allies of Germany, had any units of this brilliant German tank. At first only ten Tigers were received by Hungary, but the Germans gave them another three more on the birthday of Major General Hollósy-Kuthy. These three additional Tigers were important support for the Hungarians, who distributed them by sending two to the companies that already had the Tiger; the remainder was kept for incorporation into the training unit. Courtesy of Károly Németh.

In this picture of Tarczay in his Tiger we can see both the German emblem on the battle tank and its numeral, indicative of the 2nd Armoured Division 3/1 Battalion 2nd Company. After the supply of new armoured vehicles to Hungary by Germany, Battalion 3/1 had four companies, the 1st eleven Pz IV Hs, the 2nd six Tigers, the 3rd also six Tigers and the 4th, nine StuG IIIs. The companies that had the powerful Tigers were commanded by 1st Lieutenant Ervin Tarczay and the other by Captain János Vetress. Photo taken in Galicia in June 1944. Courtesy of Károly Németh.

Thanks to the arrival of new Zrínyi from the factories, the new Assault Gun Battalions were now fully armed. The 7th Assault Gun Battalion was in Sümeg, the 10th in Szigetvár, the 13th in Csongrád, the 16th in Debrecen, the 20th in Eger, the 24th in Kassa (Košice) and the 25th in Kolozsvár (Cluj-Napoca). In spite of this, there were not enough Zrínyi to go around, so often, they had to continue using the Toldi and Turáns.

In mid-June finally the 1st Battery of the 1st Assault Gun Battalion under the command of the 1st Lieutenant Sandor came to the front from Hajmáskér with ten Zrínyi, so for the first time the 1st Assault Gun Battalion was fully equipped on the combat front with ten vehicles per battery and one command Zrínyi.

On 13 July, the Russian army launched an offensive in the direction on Sandomierz and Lviv (Lvov) which broke the Hungarian front line. The 1st Ukrainian Front, under the command of Mariscal Koniev, acted as a battering ram against the weak

The commander of a Toldi II poses for the camera. You can see the octagonal tricolour emblem and on its right the shield of the mechanized branch of the Hungarian army. After the 38M Toldi I and due to the multitude of modifications that the Hungarians were making in the new tanks, the following 110 units manufactured between 1941 and 1942 (68 by Ganz and 42 by MÁVAG) received the denomination of 41M Toldi II. These had some improvements with respect to the previous model as the radio R-5/a and mainly that all of its components were made in Hungary. Courtesy of Károly Németh.

A damaged Toldi IIa with, in the foreground, its 40 mm weapon. It is noteworthy that carries the emblem adopted from 16 September 1942. For this new model of the Toldi, 80 Toldi IIs were used, which were rearmed with the new gun as well as other less important changes such as the replacement of the machine gun by the Gebauer 34/40AM. Courtesy of Károly Németh.

The Toldi IIa only represented a small improvement over the Toldi II, still very far from what the Hungarian armoured force required. The mediocre performance of the Toldi in action was improved by increasing its firepower and its armour (this improvement could not be carried out properly because the inability of the engine to cope with this weight gain). So in 1943, the new 42M Toldi IIa model appeared, which went from having a 20mm to a 40mm gun (the 37/42M MÁVAG that was a 40mm licensed from Bofors), and although the improvement was evident it was still completely insufficient to match the Russian forces. Courtesy of Károly Németh.

Lieutenant Barnabas Koszeghy's destroyed StuG III. He was the hero of the Hungarian assault units and the numbering identifies the vehicle as the command unit of the 7th Assault Gun Battalion. They received thirty-one StuG IIIs from the Germans, so Koszeghy left for the front at the end of August 1944 with only a few days in which to train crews in his new vehicles. Later, the 7th Assault Artillery Battalion (or Assault Gun Battalion) formed part of the 3rd Army in Arad in September of the same year. Courtesy of Károly Németh.

defensive lines of the Axis, that were made up of the Heeresgruppe Nordukraine comprising the 4th Panzer Army in the left flank, the 1st in the centre and the 1st Hungarian Army on the right. Because of this formation, the 2nd Armoured Division was put on alert and deployed urgently in Stanislau (Ivano-Frankivsk) on 23 July. The rest of the 1st Hungarian Army took shelter in the Carpathians along the incomplete fortifications of the Hunyadi line.

During the Russian offensive in July, the 1st Assault Gun Battalion suffered many casualties, which necessitated the 1st and 2nd batteries to fight a rear-guard action to slow the Russian advance to the east of Otynia. The massive Soviet

The crew of a Zrínyi II poses for the camera through its hatches in a photograph taken at a training camp in March 1944. This development of the Turán tank began with attempts by the Hungarian munitions industry to build equipment that could rival the Russians. As happened with the StuG III, the Hungarian idea was to develop two variants: one was an assault gun that would carry a 105mm howitzer; and another with a 75mm long anti-tank gun. These were used in the Zrínyi II and Zrínyi I respectively and in both cases the chassis on which they would be mounted would be that of the Turán tank. Courtesy of Károly Németh.

The lateral skirts of the Zrínyi II allowed improvement to the survival capacity during clashes with the enemy. This assault gun had 75mm armour plate at the front, 13-25mm at the sides and 25-40mm on top. These improvements were similar to those of the Turán, with side skirts although with a mesh design that did not increase the vehicle's overall weight in a similar way to the German Von Thomas armour). Courtesy of Károly Németh.

To get the most out of the lateral skirts of the Zrínyi II, it was necessary to increase the vehicle's armour and this hampered its movements. This vehicle was captured by the Russians and is on display today in the Kubinka museum. The initial production of Zrínyi II was 40 units manufactured in 1943, followed by a further 104 later. But the speed of the war meant that final production was limited to about 60 vehicles, possibly up to 66 if the Ganz factory had managed to deliver 6 more between August and September of 1944. According to Becze, the total figure was 72 units, although it is difficult to confirm that number. Curtesy of Károly Németh.

attack motivated the 1st Hungarian Army to withdraw these troops, ordering the Tigers to carry out the rear-guard movement.

From the 24th to the 29th, tanks belonging to the 2nd Armoured Division maintained continuous clashes against the Soviets along the Czuczylow-Grabevjec-Horohodina-Saturnia-Rosulna-Kraszna-Rozniatow-Dolina route. These constant clashes led to a dramatic decrease in the number of tanks in service. As an example, Battalion 3/I that lost seven Tigers in the combats, and only brought three home. It was during these battles that the legend of Ervin Tarczay was forged. He became the ace of the Hungarian armoured troops, in command of a Tiger.

At the end of the month, the Zrínyi of the 1st Assault Gun Battalion had to withstand repeated clashes with the Russians to keep open the army's escape route in the valley of Lukwa, in the direction of Rozniatow, Dolina and finally Wygoda. The 1st and 2nd batteries suffered heavy casualties during this operation, reaching the Hungarian border on 28 July through the Toronya Pass in the northeastern Carpathians along with the battalion staff.

The exhausted 2nd Armoured Division had to be removed from the front line to be reorganized in Huszt. By 9 August, the 2nd had fourteen Toldis, forty Turán-40s, fourteen Turán-75s, one Panzer III, one StuG III G and nine Pz IV Hs. They only had three Tigers left, but they would later be repaired.

Because of the deployment of the Hungarian troops in the Carpathians which acted as a natural obstacle for the advancing Russians, there was a brief lull in the fighting.

On 11 August, the Russians attacked the 1st Hungarian Army again. That was not Hungary's only concern, because on 25 August, Romania changed sides after a coup which saw them declare the war on its Hungarian neighbour, finally joining forces with the Russians to free their land of Transylvania. Faced with this new

Another image of a camouflaged Hungarian StuG III of the 7th Assault Gun Battalion, in this case with side skirts during the fighting in Hungary in 1944. This German vehicle significantly improved the effectiveness of the Hungarian armoured forces. This was amply demonstrated on 9 October 1944, when, with the help of the Zrínyi, they managed to destroy at least 67 Soviet tanks with the loss of only 10 StuG IIIs during the battle of Szentes. Courtesy of Károly Németh.

risk from the south, the 2nd Army was quickly reorganized and mobilized, with two divisions and a reserve brigade. It also had three divisions that arrived from the East and was joined by a weakened 3rd Army.

At the same time, the Russians, faced with the Hunyadi line in the Carpathians broke through the defences and marched into Hungarian territory on 27 September, facing the St. László and Árpád defensive lines. In the north, the Russians tried to force Dukla Pass on the border with Slovakia.

In the ensuing fighting in Transylvania, the following took part: the 10th Assault Gun Battalion; the armoured trains of the 101st and 102nd; and the 2nd Armoured Division that only had fourteen Toldis, forty 40M Turán 40s, fourteen 41M Turán 75s, twenty-one 40M Nimrods, twelve 39 Csabas, one Pz III, nine Pz IV Hs, three Tigers and one StuG III. On 20 September, the Germans agreed to send twenty Pz IVHs and five Panthers (the total number of Panthers in Hungary was twelve) and these were assigned to the 1st Lieutenant Tarczay's Company in the 3/I Battalion.

A Hungarian StuG III column advances towards the combat zone. The 7th Assault Gun Battalion got most of these vehicles, although other units received them too. The StuG III had a 75mm long StuK L/48 gun (Ausf.G) and although its original concept was as an assault gun, by this time it was used mainly as a tank destroyer and very effectively. Courtesy of Károly Németh.

The brand-new Toldi II prototype, with its clearly outlined mimetic scheme. After the 38M Toldi I, the Toldi II or 41M Toldi II was an improvement for the Hungarian Armoured Forces, but it was still an under-armoured and under-gunned tank and was never a match for the Soviets. Courtesy of Károly Németh.

A unique example of the Toldi prototype with the 44M rocket launcher Buzogányvető. Two types of this 100mm rocket launcher were created: an anti-tank rocket (HEAT or high explosive anti-tank) with the nickname of Buzogány (mace); and a second antipersonnel model called Zápor (rain). The first prototype of the Buzogány was manufactured and tested in the spring of 1944. It carried an explosive head of about 4kg and could pass through 300mm of armour or concrete; which made it capable of facing any Soviet tank at a distance of up to 1200m. Courtesy of Károly Németh.

Several Turán IIs ready to sent to Russia by train after capture. 139 Turán II armoured tanks were made between 1943 and 1944 but according to Németh there were 185, including some Turán Is. Courtesy of Károly Németh.

Several Hungarian soldiers are fascinated by a Panther tank. It is not known if this vehicle belonged to the Germans or the Hungarians. Fortunately, 12 of these magnificent armoured tanks arrived in Hungary, which was fortuitous since their original destiny was Romania, but when that country changed sides in 1944 the switch of vehicles was made with great efficiency. Courtesy of Károly Németh.

Another Panzer tank. In spite of documentation which describes the small numbers being used by the Hungarians, there are no known photos of Panther (Pz V) vehicles in Hungarian hands. After the Tiger, the Panther (PzV), armed with 75mm KwK 42/L70 gun and two 7.92mm MG 34 machine guns, was the most powerful fighting tank of the Hungarians. Courtesy of Károly Németh.

A Hungarian Fieseler Fi-156 plane supporting the ground troops. This German light aircraft carried out various missions like recognition, linkage, rescue and evacuation. The versatility of the 'Storch' meant that the Hungarian Royal Air Force needed to have very useful reconnaissance aircraft. FORTEPAN KONOK TAMAS ID.

Hungarian troops were largely transported by rail in Russian territory, although the Russian railway network was not very good; neither were the conditions for the troops. FORTEPAN KOKANY JENO.

A Hungarian armoured train on Soviet soil. Its presence brought mobile firepower to the Hungarian troops. In 1920, the Hungarian army had nine armoured trains, left over from before the First World War. By 1929, five of them were in such bad condition that they had to be destroyed. During the war with Russia, Hungarian trains could not be used due to the different track gauge between the two countries. But they could use armoured trains if they were captured from the Russians in the Ukraine. So between 1942 and 1944, the East Occupation Group used a train against the partisans in Bryantsk; for its part, the West Occupation Group captured an old Polish train in Upper Hungary (which had been abandoned in 1944). FORTEPAN NAGYPAL GEZA.

The Battle of Torda

On 5 September 1944, the Hungarians launched an offensive against superior Romanian forces aiming at the north of Transylvania. The spearhead was the 2nd Armoured Division and within it the powerful 2nd Company commanded by Tarczay. They crossed the Aranyos (Aires) River towards Torda (now Turda, in Romania) at dusk on 5 September beginning the Hungarian attack. The offensive was a success at first since it reached Torda ten days after it began and finally crossed the River Maros (Mures).

Romanian infantry joined the Red Army and the Romanian Armoured Division stopped the Hungarians on 9 September in their attempt to reach Transylvania's northern mountain passes.

The numerical superiority of the Romanians blocked the Hungarian advance, which forced them to retreat behind the Maros River. Here, they would form a defensive line made up of the people of Torda and Aranyosegerbegy (Viişoara).

On 10 September, Hungarian armoured troops were sent to the Reserve, although three days later they were back at the front line in Torda, where their defences were strong. Because of Torda's strategic importance, the 2nd Armoured Division could be sent as a mobile force ready to the neediest areas of the front.

On 13 and 14 September, the Russians extended their offensive to the western part of the city. Hungarian armoured troops were trying to plug the gaps made by the Russians. On the 15th, the Soviets launched their first attack on Torda after an intense artillery barrage. On the same day, the 3/I Battalion, led by their Panzer company made a successful counter-attack. In particular, Lt Taczay's Company led the attack in the eastern part of the town without waiting for the rest of his battalion or infantry units, and in this surprise manoeuvre destroyed three anti-tank cannons and wiped out two enemy infantry companies. The overwhelming superiority of the enemy meant that Tarczay's Company was surrounded but thanks to the valiant action of the Hungarian tanks they were able to escape. During the following days, led by Tarczay and his Panzers, there would be many clashes between Hungarian armour and the Russians.

The performance of the 10th Assault Artillery Battalion was outstanding in the fighting for Torda. This unit launched a successful counter-attack on the afternoon of 22 September which caught the Russians completely by surprise and blasted them with their field pieces at close range.

On 23 September, the 23rd German Panzer Division with two Panzergrenadier regiments and about 65 tanks arrived in Vaskapu and Sósfar, east-north-east of Torda. Thanks to this timely arrival, the sector held, allowing Axis troops around Torda to retreat.

On the next day, only two Panzers, six Pz IV Hs and nine Turáns from the 3rd Tank Regiment remained in fighting readiness and they were sent to the Reserve in the town of Nagy-Ördöngös. On 25 September, the number of armoured vehicles increased after repairs to the Panzers and Tigers, which went back to their original companies.

On 4 October, there were renewed Russian attacks from the west. By dusk, Torda was almost completely surrounded. The situation became so desperate that Axis troops in Transylvania had to retreat. The Romanians captured Apahida (east of Kolozsvár) clashing with Hungarian armour on 11 October.

Between 15 September and 5 October in the Torda area alone, the Panzer company destroyed eleven tanks, seventeen anti-tank cannons, twenty machine

In this famous photograph we see a shattered Hungarian Hetzer with the word Mókus (red squirrel) on its front. This vehicle, marked with identification numbers put there by the Russians, was put out of action by March 1945 in the western part of Hungary. With the 75mm L/48 gun and a 7.92mm machine gun it fought in the last defensive battles in Hungary with great success. Courtesy of Károly Németh.

guns, a rocket launcher and there were serious infantry casualties. The battle of Torda was perhaps the greatest operational success of Hungarian troops, because the ultimate goal of the Russians and their Romanian allies was to encircle their enemies in order to annihilate Army Group South. This action slowed down the Russian advance and stopped it but it led to heavy loss of destroyed and captured vehicles – the Romanians captured several Toldi, Turán, two Hetzer and at least one Zrínyi.

Continuous fighting went on in Hungarian territory. By 25 October, Tarczay was fighting in Tiszapolgár, while Hungarian troops retreating. Between 6 and 25 October, the company destroyed five tanks.

Battles in Southern Hungary

After the defection of Romania, the 4th Hungarian Corps was ordered to block the advance of Russians and Romanians across the south Hungarian plain at Arad and Lippa. To the 4th was added VII Corps, redesignated as III Army. The most powerful unit in the 4th Hungarian Corps was the 1st Armoured Division.

The Division was not up to strength because part of its armament was handed over to the 2nd Armoured Division to complete that unit. The new unit was formed in August because it was desperately needed at the front.

On 2 September the 1st Armoured Division had a tank battalion (I/III) with five Toldis in the command company, three medium-tank companies (with seven Turáns, five Toldis and thee Nímrods per company); the 1st Motorized Rifle Regiment had nine Nímrod, while the 51st self-propelled Anti-Aircraft Battalion had two command Toldis, eighteen Nímrods and three Toldis. The 1st Armoured Division had 60-70 armoured vehicles.

Under pressure from the Germans, on 13 September the Hungarians attacked, advancing from the right flank in the direction of Makó and Gyula towards Arad, but two Romanian infantry divisions and one cavalry division were waiting for them. The commander of the Third Army ordered the 1st Armoured Division to support the infantry in this attack. The capture of Arad by the evening of 13 September was the last completely independent operation of the Hungarians during the war.

Between 14-17 September, the 1st Armoured Division fought the 19th Romanian Infantry Division, breaking their defensive line on the 16th. The attack was slowed down by Russian armoured units. Despite this, on 18 September, the Hungarians had reached the foothills of the Carpathians, but now fierce resistance of the Romanians and the Russians slowed them down. A counter-attack carried out by a Russian armoured Corps and 53rd Soviet Army forced the Hungarians to fall

Side view of the prototype of 43M Lehel clearly showing its excellent design. Its creation was motivated by an urgent request in 1942 from the Hungarian Ministry of Defence because they could not get enough of the German Sd.Kfz.251/1s which would have been ideal for the task. Courtesy of Károly Németh.

A Nimrod of the 51st self-propelled Anti-Aircraft Battalion with its full crew during manoeuvres. The crew are wearing the 35M steel helmet. The 2nd Armoured Division was mobilized on 13 March 1944 and was the most powerful unit in the entire Hungarian Army. The divisional artillery was reinforced by the 1st Battalion of motorized medium howitzers equipped with the 31M 150mm guns. Something that characterized the 2nd Armoured was that all its materiel was of Hungarian origin. Its more powerful battle tanks were the 40M and 41M Turán, accompanied by the 40M Nimrod, 39M Csaba and 38M Toldi. Courtesy of Károly Németh.

back towards the Dombegyháza-Battonya line. Around twenty-three Turán and Toldi were lost during this action.

On 20 September, a joint Russian-Romanian attack supported by 40-50 tanks broke the Hungarian defensive line so that the 1st Armoured had to leave the Reserve to support the infantry. In the Lippa and Máriaradna areas, the 1st Armoured supported a Hungarian counteroffensive with the support of the 7th Assault Artillery Battalion that had eighteen StuG IIIs. It was also supported from the air the Luftwaffe, flying Stukas. In what has been called the Pénzespuszta Tank Battle, they managed to destroy about 100 Russian armoured vehicles, twenty-eight of which were T-34s.

In southern Hungary the defences were the responsibility of Army Group South under the command of General Johannes Friessner. This was added to the

A Vezér Turán (command Turán) with a dummy gun and two R-4 and one R-5/a radios. This armoured vehicle was another of the variants created from the Turán, although because of problems in the armaments industry, it could not be mass produced. Of the total production of Turán Is, twenty were modified into command tanks (Turán I P.K.) with an additional radio replacing some of the ammunition. Courtesy of Károly Németh.

An impressive image of a Nimrod of the 51st self-propelled Anti-Aircraft Battalion passing at full speed through a Russian village in 1944. The Nimrods' speed and the high rate of fire were their strengths. This Hungarian-made vehicle had six crew, a weight of 10,900kg, a main shield of 13mm thickness, a 40mm gun and a speed of 50km/h. This made it a top-class armoured vehicle, comparable in the Germany army to the Flakpanzer I Ausf. A armed with a 20mm gun. Courtesy of Péter Mujzer.

II Hungarian Army under command of General Jeno Major, and contained the 2nd Hungarian Armoured Division. The 1st Hungarian Armoured Division fought with the III Hungarian Army under the command of General József Heszlény. The VI German Army was commanded by General Maximilian Fretter-Pico.

By the 22 September, the Russians had the vast Hungarian plain in front of them. At 4.00 hours on 6 October, the 2nd Ukrainian Front began a major offensive starting from the city of Arad supported by large numbers of troops and armoured vehicles between the rivers Danube and Tisza. Without real opposition, the advance was dazzling, allowing it to penetrate 60 miles behind enemy lines during the first day. Of the many clashes between the Russians and the defenders, it is worth highlighting fighting at the Szentes bridgehead, where, among other units, was the 13th Assault Artillery Battalion with only two Turán 75s.

Despite German resistance, Russian troops crossed the Hungarian border on 8 October in the Szegez sector. During the next few days, the 1st, 13th and 23rd Panzer Divisions and the 22nd SS Cavalry Division 'Maria Theresa', temporarily stopped the Russian advance.

On 11 October, the Axis troops began a counter-offensive led by the 1st Armoured Division and the 23rd Hungarian Division, which overwhelmed the Russian advance guard in Mindszent, almost completely destroying the 4th Romanian Infantry. The Hungarian thrust was slowed on 22 October by mechanized Russian forces, which counter-attacked north of the Tisza River and pushed the Hungarians back, leaving the way open towards Debrecen and Nyíregyháza.

These battles had again bled the Hungarian troops dry. In an attempt to reorganize them, what was left of the 1st Hungarian Armoured Division, about twenty tanks by 31 October, was placed under the command of the III German Panzer Corps in Kecskemét.

Debrecen: the Gate to Budapest

The battle for Debrecen took place between 6 and 29 October. There, the Germans and Hungarians tried to stop the Russian 2nd Ukrainian Front under Malinovsky who were attempting to wipe out Hungary's eastern defences.

A Russian cavalry group penetrated the Hungarian defences as far as Debrecen. Here they encountered a powerful concentration of German forces that was concentrating in a counteroffensive called operation Zingar Baron. The idea was to push the Russians out of the Carpathians.

Among the Hungarian armoured units that took part in the defence of Debrecen was the 16th Assault Artillery Battalion equipped with ten Turán 75s and two Turán 40s. On 10 October, despite their bravery, they were forced to retreat by the Russian tanks. The next day, the Battalion, together with German infantry troops and tanks of the 23rd Panzer Division counter-attacked, stopping the Russians. This fighting continued on the 13th and 14th, slowing the Russian advance. On 19 October, the Battalion was ordered to pull back in the direction of Polgár along the Tisza River, after having lost 600 men and a lot of armoured vehicles. After the Hungarian retreat, three Romanian divisions took Debrecen between 19 and 20 October.

The Battle of Debrecen ended as a tactical victory over the Russians and Romanians who had a high number of casualties and loss of vehicles. But it had not ended Russian pressure on the battered Axis since the Soviet advance continued.

After the victory at Debrecen, the Russians and Romanians forced all German and Hungarian troops out of northern Transylvania. The Russians were advancing over German and Hungarian territory. During the second half of October, the 1st Ukrainian the 4th Ukrainian Fronts took part in the attack on Ruthenia and Slovakia.

Finally, on 29 October, the Red Army began its offensive against Budapest with more than 1 million men divided into two combat groups that converged on the capital in order to isolate it from the Axis forces still fighting in the countryside.

During the second half of November, some reinforcements of men and vehicles for the 2nd Armoured Division gradually began to arrive near Párkány (today's Sturovo in Slovakia). The 3rd Tank Regiment received nine Pz IV Hs and two Toldis; and Turán crews were trained to use the most powerful Pz IV.

The Turán II with its 75mm short weapon, represented almost the culmination of production of Hungarian war tanks in the period. After the German occupation of Hungary on 19 March 1944 the production of the Turán II became much slower and was limited exclusively to the manufacture of spare parts, rather than new vehicles. This was finished by German order in that year, finishing production just before the German invasion. Courtesy of Károly Németh.

Following the German invasion, Polish troops headed to Hungary. In this photograph are several Polish light armoured vehicles that shortly afterwards were used by the Hungarian Army, although they were obsolete by this time. FORTEPAN 78270Berkó Pál 1939.

A Hungarian Fw-190 F8 supporting Hungarian troops. On 8 November 1944, the Germans delivered sixteen Fw 190 F-8 fighters to the Hungarian Air Force. These powerful planes served with the 102nd Vadászbombázó and were used in defensive operations against American and Russian air forces and in air-to-ground operations against the Russians. FORTEPAN VARGHA ZSUZSA.

The 2nd Armoured underwent several clashes during the siege of Budapest in the Ipolyság area and were supported by a regiment of the notorious SS unit, the Sturmbrigade Dirlewanger. This area was captured by Russians on 14 December. Between 9 and 19 December the 2nd Armoured Division clashed several times in the Lovasbéreny district. By the beginning of December, the Division was practically wiped out; of 119 armoured vehicles, only 17 were still working. At full strength the vehicles were: twenty-six 40M Nímrods; eight 39M Csabas; thirty-five 40M Turán 40s; eight 41M Turán 75s; sixteen 38M Toldis; one Pz III; twenty Pz IV Hs; four Panthers (Pz v); and one StuG III. At the end of the month, the Division only had two Panthers (Pz v) and two Pz IV Hs.

A Turán crossing a bridge. The ultimate Turán was the Turán III, with side and turret skirts. Another development of the Turán was 43M Turán III, the main characteristic of which was its modified turret using a long piece of 75mm (a Hungarian copy of the German 7.5 cm Pak 40 called 75mm 43 M L/55); as well as bettter shielding. FORTEPAN 130014 Lázár György.

A prototype assembled from the Turán III battle tank tower. Only one was built, in February 1944, which marked the zenith of the development of the Hungarian armoured tank and, had it been mass produced, it would have constituted a dangerous threat to the Russians. Courtesy of Károly Németh.

Several Hungarian soldiers surround a captured Russian T-34/76. Few could of these be modified for service against their original owners. Some T-34s were painted with the Hungarian cross to avoid confusion and were used against the Russians from 1942. Because of the small number of T-34s captured by the Hungarians there was a serious spare part problem. They were unable to face the huge military capacity of the Red Army. FORTEPAN.

A photograph of a Russian armoured train put out of action. Some of these would later be reused. In late 1944 and early 1945 Hungarian trains were used in fighting around Budapest and Lake Balaton. In the capital, three armoured trains were involved, based on the Keleti station. From their position in the different branches of railway tracks they were used as artillery points because of their 80mm guns. FORTEPAN TELLER FERENC.

One of the few half-tracks Sd.Kfz.251/8 in its medical support version. This is among other vehicles in the Automobile depot in 1942. There is evidence that the 2nd Armoured Division had one of these ambulances at the end of 1944 bearing the emblem of the Red Cross and it is also possible that some other Sd.Kfz.251s ambulances were used by the Hungarians after 1942. FORTEPAN Lissák Tidavar 1943.

A close-up of a Csaba tankette that served so well during the war. The vehicle on the left is a Strauler ACII still waiting for its guns to be fitted at the Automobile Depot. The main armament was the 36mm Solothurn 20mm gun and an 8mm machine gun, both located in a centrally arranged turret. A second machine gun was positioned in the rear hatch as anti-aircraft protection but could also be used in reconnaissance by the crew on foot. FORTEPAN Lissák Tidavar.

The Siege of Budapest

The attack on the Hungarian capital began on 29 October and by 7 November the Russians had reached the outer suburbs about 20km. Preparations for the siege of city centre began on 9 December and the bombardment opened up on the 19th.

Several units of the 1st Armoured and Hussars Division with what was left of the 6th Assault Artillery Battalion were besieged in the city. Among the German troops were the remains of the 13th Panzer Division, the 60th Panzergrenadier Division 'Feldherrnhalle', 8th SS Cavalry Division 'Florian Geyer' and the 22nd SS Cavalry Division 'Maria Theresa'.

The 1st Armoured Division had seven tanks and three anti-tank guns and the 1st Hussars Division had only four armoured vehicles. The 6th Assault Artillery Battalion made up of 1st, 7th, 10the and parts of the 13th, 16th and 25th Companies were integrated in the 'Group Billnitzer' with thirty assault artillery vehicles (StuG III, Zrínyi and Hetzer) and eight 75mm anti-tank guns. There were also some newly manufactured Zrínyi made by the Ganz factory that was still operating in the city. As there were many more troops than vehicles, many of the troops fought with the infantry.

The 10th Assault Artillery Battalion and a battery of the 1st Battalion carried out a counter attack on a Russian bridgehead in Baracska on 8 December, which drove the Russians back to Ercsi on the Danube. Just three days later, the battery of the 1st Assault Artillery Battalion and vehicles belonging to 10th Assault Artillery Battalion were fighting in the streets of the city of Erd to the south-west of Budapest.

We should remember the efforts of the gendarmerie who fought with the armour in Budapest. They had ten obsolete Ansaldo, taken out of action years before, ten Toldis and ten Csabas. The units carried out attacks on the Soviet troops in Vecsés on 1 November 1, but the results were disastrous.

During November and December, the Assault Artillery Battalions fought on foot in the Vecsés-Maglad-Ecser districts of Pest, alongside the 1st Hungarian Armoured Division. The constant attacks and counter-attacks were repeated along the whole front, resulting in the gain or loss of a few hundred metres each time.

The attack from the east increased the pressure on the defenders every day. Thus on 28 December most of 'Group Billnitzer' found itself trapped in the Kispest area. On the same day, after unsuccessful attempts to stop the enemy offensive, the remains of the 1st and 13th Hungarian Assault Artillery Battalions between Pécel and Ferihegy had to retreat, unable to close the gap left by the 8th SS Cavalry Division 'Florian Geyer'. On the other hand, armoured units of the 16th and 24th Assault Artillery Battalions held their positions in Rákoskeresztur and Újmajor. On the same day, Maglód and Gyál, to the south-east of Pest, were already in Russian hands. On 31 December, armoured vehicles belonging to 24th Assault Artillery Battalion commanded by Barnabas Bakó halted a Russian attack inflicting heavy casualties at Rakóskeresztúr.

In the face of the imminent arrival of the attackers in the city centre, the 'Group Billnitzer' was ordered to block the Grand Boulevard, the fifth barricade that the defenders had set up, with armoured vehicles and crews that could still fight. The new Russian offensive forced the defenders to fall back on Buda and the 'Group Billnitzer' were ordered to stem the advance. For its part, the 1st Armoured Division had lost all its vehicles so the men joined the infantry for the rest of the siege.

On 25 January, armoured vehicles belonging to 'Group Billnitzer' with German infantry tried to capture a munitions factory in the railway area around Lágymános. By 11 February, frustrated by the failure of operations Konrad I, II and III, the city's commandant, SS-Obergruppenführer von Wildenbruch, ordered all his forces to break the siege by any means. What was left of 'Group Billnitzer', without their armour, took part in an escape from Castle Hill. Only a few of them reached the safety of German lines after serious fighting.

Remains of Lieutenant Tibor Rácz's Zrínyi II of the 3rd Battery of the 1st Assault Gun Battalion in a Budapest avenue (Vérmezö). The photograph was taken after the end of the armed conflict. The 'Billnitzer' Group consisted of the remains of the battalions that had withdrawn from the front to the city, which were those of the 1st, 7th, 10th and parts of the 13th, 16th and 25th (according to some historians, a battery from 20th with Hetzer should also be added and the rest of 24th with five Turán, two Toldi and twenty-two Hetzer). Tibor Rácz tried to escape from Budapest but he was shot and killed. Courtesy of Károly Németh.

A captured Hungarian StuG III, with identification numbers painted by the Russians. During the fighting at the Szentes bridgehead in October 1944, most of the 7th Assault Gun Battalion was destroyed. What was left fled towards Budapest, where they joined the 'Billnitzer' Group. In the Battalion's defence, they destroyed at least 67 tanks and 14 vehicles of various types during the clashes with the Russians in the Tisza River area. They lost eight StuG IIIs destroyed, ten with severe damage and twelve with light damage. Courtesy of Károly Németh.

A civilian reads a newspaper account about the destruction of a Zrínyi II of the 'Billnitzer' Group in Budapest shortly after the end of the war. The remains of six assault battalions led by Lieutenant General Ernö Billnitzer, head of the training camp, had a total of about thirty assault guns (StuG III, Zrínyi and Hetzer) and eight anti-tank 75mm guns. Since there were more troops than vehicles, many of the crews were used as infantry troops. The Zrínyi and the Hetzer were very useful because of their low silhouette and powerful guns in the street fight that awaited them. Even so, in the defence of Budapest, they were very inferior to the Russians. FORTEPAN.

The Erzsébet bridge in Pest being demolished to slow the Russian advance. When the Hungarian and German soldiers withdrew from Pest the plan was to concentrate defences in Buda. Accordingly, the five bridges across the Danube were attacked on January 18 at 7 o'clock in the morning to make it more difficult for the Russians to advance. The only two that remained standing despite serious damage were the Erzsébet and the Chains bridges. The 'Billnitzer' Group was immediately deployed in the western part of Buda. FORTEPAN KRAMER ISTVAN DR.

A Turán II armoured tank runs through the streets of Budapest. During the siege of the city, the 1st Armoured Division had seven tanks, three anti-tank guns and about 5000 men. The 1st Hussar Division had only four armoured vehicles. The six assault tank battalions led by Lieutenant General Ernö Billnitzer had a total of about thirty assault guns (StuG IIIs, Zrínyis and Hetzers) and eight 75mm anti-tank guns. FORTEPAN BERKO PAL.

Numerous panzerfaust accumulated in a trench in the defence of Budapest. In the absence of more armoured vehicles, the defenders of the city used this devastating anti-tank weapon in large quantities. On 5 January, Russian tanks were already in some areas of Pest, although it is true that many areas of that part of the city were still in the hands of their defenders. On the 6th, the Russians took the Hofherr-Schrantz factory, which was the only one that still manufactured spare parts for the German-Hungarian armoured vehicles and could carry out repairs. FORTEPAN 60130

Remains of the fighting in the streets of Budapest. The situation was desperate in the Hungarian capital, since all chance of help from outside disappeared, frustrated by operations Konrad I, II and III. The commandant of the city, SS-Obergruppenführer von Wildenbruch ordered the barricades to be broken on 11 February. To try to take the Russians by surprise and have some chance of success, the siege was breached in three directions. There were between 28,000 and 30,000 German and Hungarian soldiers involved. Only the first managed to advance a certain distance sheltering in the fog, while the other two were massacred. FORTEPAN UNGVARY KRISZTIAN.

After the horrors of the siege came the Russian occupation of Budapest. The siege officially ended on 14 February 1945 when the Russians decisively defeated the last German-Hungarian defences. Of the defending force, only about 600 or 700 Germans and a few dozen Hungarians managed to escape, reaching the defensive lines outside Vienna. FORTEPAN 58306

Chapter Six

The Swansong of the Hungarian Armoured Forces, 1945

In early January 1945, a small combat group from the 2nd Armoured Division was put under the command of the Szent László Division which took part in the battle of Garam River. The 3rd Tank Regiment had three 38M Toldis and two Pz IV Hs. The 52nd self-propelled Anti-Aircraft Artillery Battalion had seven 40M Nimrods. It is possible that all the Zrínyis still operational in the various Assault Artillery Battalions were transferred to the 20th and 24th during the month.

On 1 January, Tarczay was promoted to captain after which he was entrusted with the mission of moving with forty of his men to Galánta, where they collected new armoured vehicles a week later. These were twenty-seven Pz IV Hs (and according to some sources two Panzers) which would boost the firepower of the 2nd Armoured Division.

In order to liberate Budapest, Operation Konrad was developed in three phases. Hungarian involvement in these operations was quite marginal, the most important being the action of the 2nd Armoured Division with fifteen Pz IV Hs and some other vehicles, in Operation Konrad I between 7 and 12 January in Székesfehérvár. On 16 January, the 2nd Armoured, already reinforced with twenty-seven Pz IV Hs, in addition to five Nímrods, one Panzer and some other vehicles was ready for action.

On the 24th, the unit, together with the 4th German Cavalry Brigade, supported the attack of the 1st Hussars Division in the Vértes Mountains. The Hungarians attacked in Csákvár with eleven Pz IV Hs and four Nimrods.

These continuous clashes destroyed the few remaining armoured vehicles of the 2nd Armoured Division. At the end of February, they tried to form a defensive line near Székefehérvár and Zámoly, beside Lakes Balaton and Velence. 3/II Tank Battalion with fifteen Pz IV H fought against vastly superior Soviet troops in Zámoly. The unit, with sixteen Pz IV Hs, four batteries and four Motorized Battalions was put under the command of the IV SS Armoured Corps.

On 17 March, Tarczay, with four Pz IV Hs faced twenty Russian Sherman tanks near the village of Söréd and the Hungarian hero was killed during the retreat. Despite the critical situation, Hungarian armoured units still kept a good number of vehicles in service. Part of the 25th Assault Artillery Battalion was still fighting during March, although only six of its thirty-eight guns were operative.

The last attempt to stop the Russian advance in Hungary was called Operation Spring Awakening (Unternehmen Frühlingserwachen) and is also known as the Lake Balaton offensive. Hungarian armour did not take part in this. One of the last Hungarian armoured units still fighting, the 20th Assault Artillery Battalion, only had eight Hetzers still working. After a number of clashes with the Russians, the Battalion was taken out of the front line. In the last two months of the war, Hungarian armoured vehicles still fighting did so in small numbers scattered in various parts of the front. On 21 March, the last operating Zrínyi, belonging to the 24th Assault Artillery Battalion, surrendered in Bratislava, Slovakia, as well as a handful of Turán I survivors.

The speed of the Russian attack and the lack of fuel caused during the escape to the north of the country meant that some of the few Hungarian armoured vehicles were abandoned still in fighting condition. Győr, the second largest city in Hungary, fell on 28 March. The next day, the Prime Minister, Ferenc Szálasi, and his government left Hungary and fled to Austria. Even so, some Axis forces carried on fighting in Hungary until at least 12 April 12. By then, the whole of Hungary was occupied by the Russians but three small areas still held out. What was left of the 1st Army was in Slovakia and retreated to Bohemia, where they finally surrendered to the Russians. The 3rd Army, where the 2nd Armoured Division were still fighting, was in Austria along the north bank of the Danube; they surrendered to the Western Allies. Finally, several mixed units like the 'Szent László' were forced to leave northern Croatia, where they were fighting against Marshal Tito's Communist partisans, for Austria, where they surrendered to the British. As a curious footnote, the British allowed the men of the 'Szent László' to keep their weapons in their fight against Tito.

The only existing photograph of the 15cm Nebelwerfer rocket launcher prototype on a Zrínyi II. Another version incorporated the 150 mm rocket launcher Nebelwerfer 41 into the Zrínyi II. Had it been manufactured in large enough numbers, the Hungarian army would have acquired much needed firepower that it lacked throughout the war. It would have held a similar position as that of the Nebelwerfer in the German army, allowing a great capacity of movement and firepower. Courtesy of Károly Németh.

The German and Hungarian withdrawal was carried out in appalling weather conditions, with snow and mud hampering operations. This situation was taken advantage of by the Russians as well as by partisan troops in Czech territory, who attacked Axis soldiers. Particular examples are the 1st Hungarian Armoured Division or the 20th Assault Tank Battalion. This constant harassment coupled with the lack of fuel for vehicles meant that much armoured materiel was abandoned by the roadside still in perfect working order. This was particularly true in Zaim (Znojmo) on the Czech-Austrian border and at the railway station of Budafok-Háros.

Conclusions

Hungary's role in the Second World War was complicated, particularly in the context of Romania, for centuries an enemy, that became, in this war, an ally. During the war, Hungary organized its mobile forces, and developed its own military industry that was able to supply armaments and equipment for its troops. The munitions industry was able to produce all kinds of weapons and armoured vehicles. However, Hungarian armoured vehicles were outdated from the very moment they were supplied, being inferior to the Russian vehicles during all phases of the war. Hungary's only top level armoured vehicles, like the Tigers and Panzers, were provided by Germany but were not available in sufficient numbers to make an impact.

The Hungarian armoured troops were faced by one of the most formidable armies of the day, the Red Army. Technical failures and tactics were evident from the beginning of operations. However, the troops did their best against all odds. They went into combat knowing that even the heaviest anti-tank weapon they had had very little chance against the Russian T-34. In spite of this, these men fought until the end, when Hungary was already in enemy hands.

After the war, only a few members of the Hungarian Army joined a new force, the so-called Democratic Army but most of them were demobilized and went home. The less fortunate were those who were arrested and interned for years or in some cases executed by the Communist regime.

As a result of the final defeat, between 419,000 and 600,000 Hungarians were deported to Siberian labour camps. Approximately 40 per cent of them (at least 200,000) would never come home. The survivors returned to Hungary between 1953 and 1956. In terms of territory, Hungarian possessions were the same as in 1938, except for a small territorial loss on its border with Czechoslovakia. All the annexations that took place between 1938-41 and the country's hopes of rebuilding a Greater Hungary had been destroyed for ever.

I hope that this text will bring Hungary's story to a wider audience and reflect the bravery of the Hungarian army faced with impossible difficulties.

Bibliography

Becze, Csaba, *Magyar Steel*, Stratus, 2006.

Bernád, Denes; Kliment, Charles K., *Magyar Warriors: The History of the Royal Hungarian Armed Forces 1919-1945*, Volume I, Helion & Company, 2015.

Bernád, Denes; Kliment, Charles K., *Magyar Warriors: The History of the Royal Hungarian Armed Forces 1919-1945*, Volume II, Helion & Company, 2017.

Bonhardt, Attila, *Zrínyi II Assault Howitzer*, PeKo Publishing, 2015.

Gil Martínez, Eduardo Manuel, *Fuerzas acorazadas húngaras 1939-45*, Almena, 2017.

Mc Taggart, Patrick, *¡Asedio!*, Inédita Editores SL, 2010.

Mujzer, Péter, *Huns on Wheels*, Mujzer & Partner Ltd.

Mujzer, Péter, *Hungarian Armored Forces in World War II*, Kagero 2017.

Order of battle and handbook of the Hungarian armed forces. February 1944, USA War Department.

Thomas, Nigel; Pál Szábo, László, *The Royal Hungarian Army in World War II*, Osprey Publishing, 2008.

Zaloga, Steven J., *Tanks of Hitler's Eastern Allies 1941-45*, Osprey Publishing, 2013.

Web wot-news, Hungarian armor part 1 – 7, Por Silentstalker and Károly "Karika" Németh, 2013-2014.

Web wot-news, Hungarian Marder – The Toldi páncélvadász project, Károly "Karika" Németh, 2014.